Oloketa Tingting Fo Apem Education Long Solomon Islands

Issues in Solomon Islands Education

Editor: Noeline Alcorn

NZCER PRESS

Wellington 2010

NZCER PRESS
New Zealand Council for Educational Research
PO Box 3237
Wellington
New Zealand

© Noeline Alcorn, 2010

ISBN 978-1-877398-91-9

All rights reserved

Designed by Cluster Creative
Cover image by Donn Ratana
Printed by Printlink, Wellington

Distributed by NZCER Distribution Services
PO Box 3237
Wellington
New Zealand
www.nzcer.org.nz

Contents

Introduction	9
SECTION ONE Systemic Issues	15
Chapter 1 Educational Decentralisation: The Growth of Community High Schools in the Solomon Islands	17
Introduction	17
The research investigation	19
The initial establishment of CHS	19
What factors influenced the establishment of CHS?	*19*
Consultation processes in establishing CHS	*22*
The ongoing operation of CHS	23
The availability and sufficiency of financial and other support for CHS	*23*
The administration of CHS	*26*
Issues and problems facing CHS	30
To what extent have CHS achieved their goals?	33
Conclusions	36
References	38
Chapter 2 The Educational and Career Aspirations Solomon Islands' Parents Hold for Their Children	41
Introduction	41
Secondary education in the Solomon Islands	42
Parents' perceptions of education	43
Parents' educational and career aspirations for their children	44
The research design	46
The findings	47
Parents' educational and career aspirations for their children	*47*
Parents' understanding of the Solomon Islands education system	*52*
Parents' views of vocational education	*54*
Some concluding thoughts	55
References	57

Chapter 3 Mi Wanfala Tisa Nao, Bata!: Beginning Secondary Teachers' Professional Learning in the Solomon Islands	**61**
Introduction	61
Context	62
Method	64
Findings	65
Sense of preparedness	*65*
Perceptions about their ITE	*66*
Induction experiences	*69*
Professional learning experiences	*72*
Discussion	74
Key findings	75
Initial teacher education experiences	*75*
Induction and professional learning experiences	*76*
Implications for educational researchers, policy makers, teacher educators and school leaders	78
Conclusion	82
References	83
SECTION TWO School Leadership	**85**
Chapter 4 Effective School Leadership in the Solomon Islands	**87**
Introduction	87
The research process	88
The findings: Issues affecting school leadership	89
Systemic issues	*89*
Systemic policy issues	95
Sociocultural and community issues	*96*
Conclusion	97
References	100
Chapter 5 Highly Effective School Principalship in the Solomon Islands	**103**
Introduction	103
Research design	105
Perceptions of highly effective principalship in the Solomon Islands	106
Links between traditional Solomon Islands leadership and principalship	*106*
Issues impeding effective principalship	*107*
Discussion and significance of the findings	108
Professional relationships	*109*
Individual qualities of a leader	*109*
Managing, leading and becoming knowledgeable	*110*

Leading as role modelling	*111*
Issues that impede highly effective principalship	*112*
Conclusion	116
References	117

Chapter 6 Seen But Not Heard: The Educational Leadership Experiences of Women Leaders in Solomon Islands Secondary Schools — **121**

Introduction	121
Research methodology and process	123
Leadership experiences of the women in the study	124
Getting appointed	*124*
Feeling a lack of confidence	*125*
Balancing work and family	*127*
Violence against women	*129*
Discrimination	*130*
Lack of initial preparation, leadership training and ongoing professional learning	*131*
Lack of consultation in the decision-making process	*132*
What can be done to facilitate women's leadership in Solomon Islands secondary schools?	133
Allowing women to lead in their own way	*133*
Providing access to education and professional development for women	*134*
Acknowledging the influence of culture and gender on attitudes towards women leaders	*136*
Conclusion	138
References	140

SECTION THREE Wider Curriculum Issues — **145**

Chapter 7 Really Useful Knowledge — **147**

Introduction	147
Educational aims and outcomes in developing countries	148
The Solomon Islands' context: Theorising about really useful knowledge	150
Increased critical and political awareness	*152*
The creation of a skilled and competent paid workforce	*153*
Improved health	*153*
Investigating educators' views	154
Changes in Solomon Islands education since 2004	156
Curriculum Development Centre	*157*
Technology curriculum	*157*
Teacher education partnership	*158*
Untrained teachers	*158*
Emphasis on quality	*159*

Continued growth and support for CHS: Access, community ownership and curriculum	*159*
Co-ordination between education sectors	*160*
Conclusion	161
References	162

Chapter 8 The Impact of Effective Professional Development on Technical Education in the Solomon Islands — **165**

Introduction	165
Context	167
Methods	168
Findings	169
The preliminary inquiry	*169*
The intervention programme	*172*
Discussion	175
Conclusion	177
References	178

Chapter 9 Technology Teachers' Perceptions of Access to and Use of ICT Tools in Solomon Islands Schools — **181**

Introduction	181
Context	182
Research design	183
Participants' profiles	*184*
Data collection	*184*
Key findings	185
Limitations to access to and use of ICT in schools	*185*
Limited ICT infrastructure and resources in the schools and the impact on teacher use of ICT	*186*
Teachers' use of ICT tools	*188*
Low level of ICT knowledge and skills	*189*
The need for policies on ICT use in schools	*190*
Teachers' beliefs about the benefits of ICT	*191*
The need for professional development in ICT	*192*
Significance of the findings	193
Teachers' access to ICT	*193*
Teachers' use of ICT tools	*194*
Teachers' level of ICT knowledge and skill	*195*
The development of policies and guidelines for ICT use in schools	*196*
Future challenges	197
Conclusion	199
References	200

Chapter 10 Attitudes to Inclusive and Special Education in the Solomon Islands	**203**
Introduction	203
The evolution of inclusive education	205
Background to this study	207
Perceptions of special and inclusive education among teacher education students and teacher educators	208
Issues arising from the findings	211
A possible way forward	213
References	216

Introduction

This book is the outcome of a partnership between the School of Education, Solomon Islands College of Higher Education (SICHE), and the Faculty of Education at the University of Waikato. The partnership, funded by New Zealand's International Aid and Development Agency to build capacity in the School of Education, began in mid-2006 and will formally end at the end of 2010, although the strong links and relationships between the staff at the two institutions will continue.

An important goal of the partnership was to begin developing a research culture within the School of Education. This has occurred in many different ways, including evidence-based practice, programme evaluations, and encouraging students to read more widely in educational literature. Here we found a singular lack of resources that directly address issues of Solomon Islands education, with the exception of two recent titles from He Parekereke at Victoria University of Wellington.[1] Almost all the chapters in this book refer to the lack of local material in their area of investigation. It was this lack of indigenous resources that resulted in the use of inappropriate texts and readings in schools and higher education during the mission era, but also since greater state involvement after independence.

A number of staff at the School of Education, the Ministry of Education and Human Resources Development (MEHRD), the Curriculum Development Centre and SICHE have studied for masters and doctoral degrees in other countries—Australia, New Zealand, Fiji and the United States—before returning to take up leadership positions in the Solomon Islands. As part of their studies they carried out research projects that resulted in the completion of academic theses. These theses contain invaluable material that was largely inaccessible to a wider audience, even though they reported on field work carried out in the Solomon Islands and the interviews on which the research was based had been conducted in pidgin. The length, complexity, academic language and unpublished nature of the theses meant that few readers were able to access them. Through the partnership, we conceived the idea of publishing a book that contained chapters from a range of these theses, all of them examining and illuminating aspects of Solomon Islands education, in order to make the research findings available to policy makers, teachers and students.

A number of Solomon Islands researchers were invited to take part in the project, though not all were able to accept. In the end, all those who contributed were graduates of the University of Waikato, which gave added emphasis to the importance of the partnership. Over a period of two years there has been ongoing conversation and mutual support as the writing progressed and the book took shape. Like their counterparts, who are emerging researchers and writers in New Zealand, the Solomon Islands academics did not find it easy to plan time for writing, did not see themselves as writers and were hesitant about their capacity to become published authors. This book is a testimony to their talent and hard work.

The 10 chapters in the book have been organised in three sections. The first section discusses systemic issues, including teacher education. It begins with a chapter on what is perhaps the most significant development in Solomon Islands education over the past 15 years: the establishment and rapid growth of community high schools, which have resulted in both local ownership and greatly increased participation in secondary education. Derek Sikua's doctoral thesis drew on his experience as Permanent Secretary for Education and his wide reading in decentralisation around the world, complemented by an extensive series of interviews. His chapter (co-written with Noeline Alcorn) shows the complexity of the process of developing the new schools, their success (as measured by exponential growth, initiated by local communities), and the need for resourcing and clear policies.

The second chapter, by Rose Beuka and Jane Strachan, investigates the aspirations Solomon Islands parents hold for their children's education. In her research Rose found that parents want schools to prepare their children for careers that will provide financial security and can be undertaken in both urban and rural locations. Although academic education is highly valued, practical skills are seen as necessary and she argues for secondary schools to offer a wide range of subjects. In the third chapter, Patricia Rodie writes of the self-perceptions new secondary teachers hold about their training and induction. Although they feel generally confident in their roles, all of them identified problem areas. Their main sources of support were other teachers and Curriculum Development Centre workshops, and they were hampered by heavy workloads and a lack of resources.

In Section two of the book three writers examine issues of school leadership, which they see as key to raising educational standards and implementing change. Donald Malasa and Collin Ruqebatu explore what effective leadership would look like and identify barriers to its achievement. Shalom Akao investigates the experiences of female educational leaders and the reasons why becoming a female leader in the Solomon Islands is so difficult. All three stress the need for leadership training and professional development for new and established leaders, calling for these leaders to be encouraged to consider wider educational issues and theoretical frameworks for leadership, as well as developing social, cultural and political awareness. They also emphasise the need for ongoing support and the provision of resources for school leaders.

The third section focuses on wider curriculum issues. Susanne Maezama, whose thesis analyses what "really useful knowledge" would look like in a Solomon Islands context, updates her work by examining current developments. David Sade investigates the impact of professional development on teachers to help them implement the new technology curriculum, which depends on technological understanding and active student learning through problem solving. Solomon Pita explores teachers' perceptions of IT and the extent to which they are able to integrate it into their teaching practices. Finally, Janine Simi examines student and lecturer understanding of special and inclusive education, and finds that students are totally ignorant of the concepts. She argues that key concepts and strategies should be addressed in initial teacher education and wider changes made to incorporate inclusion in national educational policy.

The process of putting together the book has been a collaborative one and a learning experience for all those involved. Our communication has straddled cultural differences and understanding, differing expectations and aspirations, and has had to contend with uncertain Internet connections and phone lines that do not always work. Some chapters were jointly written by Solomon Islands and Waikato colleagues. The publication is a testimony to the commitment and determination of all the talented and knowledgeable contributors to make time for the project in the midst of busy lives. It is my hope that it will serve a real need by providing information and challenging thinking, and that it will also inspire others to believe they too can publish their work for a wider audience.

My special thanks go to Dr Joanna Daiwo of the School of Education, SICHE, who provided support for the earlier stages of the project, and to Susanne Maezama, Head of School, for her input to the project and for herself being a contributor to the book. Associate Professor Jane Strachan, the Partnership Director, has been both inspirational and supportive. She also assisted directly with the writing of Chapter 2. Professor Alister Jones, Dean of the Faculty of Education, provided moral support and financial backing for the publication. I am also grateful to Robyn Baker and Bev Webber from NZCER for their enthusiastic support of the book proposal and their conviction that the project is a worthwhile one.

Noeline Alcorn
Emeritus Professor
University of Waikato
Hamilton
New Zealand

---

1 K. Sanga & K. Walker. (2005). *Apem moa: Solomon Islands leadership*. Wellington: He Parekereke, Victoria University of Wellington; K. Sanga & C. Chu. (2009). *Living and leaving a legacy of hope: Stories by new generation Pacific leaders*. Wellington: He Parekereke, Victoria University of Wellington.

SECTION ONE

SYSTEMIC ISSUES

CHAPTER 1
Educational Decentralisation: The Growth of Community High Schools in the Solomon Islands

Derek Sikua
Solomon Islands Parliament

Noeline Alcorn
University of Waikato, Hamilton, New Zealand

Introduction

Concern about access to secondary education in the Solomon Islands became acute in the early 1990s. In 1993 the country had one of the lowest coverage and completion rates at secondary level in the world, with the participation of girls particularly problematic (World Bank, 1993). Only a small percentage of primary students (26 percent) were able to go on to secondary schools, with 74 percent suffering "pushout" because there was no capacity to maintain them in the system. The literacy rate of the Solomon Islands' population was only 27 percent. Yet since independence in 1978 there has been an increasing need for citizens with higher levels of literacy and general education.

As a result, the Solomon Islands Government began exploring options for providing secondary education other than the traditional and expensive boarding schools, which require students to incur high travel and accommodation costs, often involving travel outside their own province. During the early 1990s the Government sought assistance from the World Bank and bilateral donors to fund five junior secondary day schools as a pilot programme. The enthusiastic response to these schools spurred the then Minister to take a paper to Cabinet in 1994 seeking approval to open more government- and community-funded and supported community high schools (CHS). Subsequently, over 95 CHS were established throughout the country.

The development of CHS raised issues about educational decentralisation in the Solomon Islands and the integration of educational administration between national, provincial and local levels. Making sure that responsibilities are divided appropriately, but that adequate control of decentralised tasks and support functions is maintained, would be challenging (Habu, 1983). Unnecessary bureaucracy and very long communication channels needed to be eliminated while ensuring central oversight of quality. Consultants' reports stressed the need for provincial education officers to have suitable training to enable them to implement change and work with the Ministry of Education and Human Resources Development (MEHRD) (Doyle, 1983; Thomas, 1983).

This chapter presents the findings from a sustained research project investigating the development and operation of CHS and identifies issues they raise at all levels of the system. It investigates their establishment, their ongoing operation and administration, issues and problems, and finally considers the extent to which they have achieved their goals. We conclude that decentralisation is an appropriate model for Solomon Islands secondary education because it has increased access, efficiency and local support for education. However, we argue that its continued success will depend on the extent to which five criteria for sustainability in a developing country are addressed.

The research investigation

This research was carried out with the benefit of an Overseas Development Aid (ODA) scholarship to New Zealand while Derek Sikua was on leave from his position as Permanent Secretary of MEHRD, after a career as a secondary teacher and public servant. In these roles he was confronted with the country's ongoing problems in the education sector, where access, quality, equity, efficiency and co-ordination are major issues. His overriding concern was to seek ways to address these sectoral issues so that as many Solomon Islands children as possible could receive more and better education.

To investigate the problem he studied a range of policy documents, files and reports in MEHRD and carried out one-to-one interviews with over 50 people in Guadalcanal, Isabel, Western and Central provinces, at the national, provincial, school and community levels. He observed the work of officials, teachers and school committee members and visited six case study schools in action. A second round of interviews in 2000 to check the initial findings was hampered by ongoing social tensions, but he was able to get detailed questionnaire responses from 31 of the original interviewees. In preparation for the research, he studied reports and scholarly writing on various forms of decentralisation and community developments in a range of other countries.

The initial establishment of CHS

What factors influenced the establishment of CHS?

In the early 1990s there was overwhelming agreement in the Solomon Islands that the lack of secondary places was a major concern, not only for central government and education officials but also for parents, who were often upset and angry that their children "failed" to get a secondary place. Some parents cried when the examination results were announced, and others tried to assault teachers, thinking they were to blame rather than the system. The rapidly rising population made the situation worse, as each year the number of dropouts grew. The establishment of CHS was seen as a response to this situation. Most people interviewed also believed that the new schools would assist girls to attend secondary school. The boarding schools had often lacked sufficient female dormitories, and many parents were reluctant to send their daughters away to a place where they would be separated from their traditional cultural beliefs and might be alienated from village life and obligations. Being able to attend a day school close to home would allow parents to remain a major influence for their daughters.

There was also a perceived need to improve the existing imbalances in secondary school places among the provinces, and to combat the effect of the country's geography and scattered population. More than 84 percent of the population lived in over 6,000 villages. This led to growing dissatisfaction in rural areas, since the existing secondary schools were mainly in major centres such as Honiara, Auki and Gizo. Some participants in the survey hoped that the establishment of CHS would reduce rural–urban drift and stop the alienation from their own culture that often affected students who had attended high school away from home. Officials and parents hoped that CHS would promote the teaching and learning of local cultures and languages. It was also felt that other community members might be able to use the facilities for classes in literacy, family planning and other training classes, especially (perhaps) for women.

Another major reason for the establishment of CHS was to reduce costs. Although the Government was anxious to extend secondary education, its financial situation did not allow it to do so through traditional channels. Boarding schools incur high costs for transport, accommodation and food; day schools do not. CHS would be cheaper to build, as parents and communities could offer free labour and materials for the construction of classrooms and staff houses. Parents in turn would be spared the expenses of travel to distant schools, clothes and fees. Provincial authorities felt that this would enable poorer families to allow their children to attend.

It was expected that the establishment of CHS would foster a feeling of ownership and pride within local communities. The new ventures would be partnerships between central government, provincial education authorities, schools and communities. However, a number of those interviewed saw the need for greater clarity about the responsibilities of each member of the partnership. Some felt that greater decentralisation was needed, others that MEHRD ought to exert greater control. One area of disagreement was the selection of pupils, which a number of schools thought should be done locally. Another was teacher discipline. Overall, the lack of necessary skills such as financial management, organisational ability, communication skills and knowing how to work effectively with adults at the school and community level was seen as a barrier to greater devolution by government.

External forces also played a role at the government level, though most of those interviewed for the research were unaware of this. The five World Bank-funded CHS provided an impetus for further development and made stakeholders at various levels aware of new possibilities for development. Reports conducted for the MEHRD with World Bank funding tended to focus on lowering the cost of education per student and involving lower level bodies in the decision-making process, rather than relying solely on central planning (World Bank, 1993). Internationally, decentralisation was seen as the answer to a range of educational issues, although the rationale behind it varied. This research project aimed to explore its cultural and geographic appropriateness in a Melanesian country such as the Solomon Islands.

Consultation processes in establishing CHS

Most writers on decentralisation (e.g., Fiske, 1996; Rondinelli, 1981) stress the need for all parties concerned to consult each other fully and develop clearly understood processes. This study found that in the establishment of CHS in the Solomon Islands, the officially approved processes were not sufficiently understood or followed. The MEHRD was put under a great deal of pressure from communities—and sometimes by local politicians—to approve new schools where the basic facilities had not been put in place or the locations were unsuitable. There are important lessons to be learnt from the experience. It is vital that consultation procedures be fully understood and agreed to *before* the implementation of new policies (Fiske, 1996). However, these policies should be flexible enough to cater for differing situations and to meet the needs of communities without stifling initiatives (Bray, 1987; Rondinelli, 1981).

The official consultation procedure drawn up and adopted by the MEHRD, following Cabinet approval in November 1994 to establish CHS, involved MEHRD officials having several meetings in areas earmarked for CHS expansion to explain the necessary requirements for approval and establishment. Thus several consultative meetings with teachers, administrators and community members were held in Isabel province and around Honiara. These meetings eventually resulted in three schools in Isabel and six in Honiara. Following this success, the MEHRD planned to open five CHS a year for the next five years, following consultation in the other eight provinces.

However, the grassroots enthusiasm for the concept of CHS was so high that the official consultation process was often not followed. In fact, over one-third of those who completed the questionnaire were unaware of the process. Forty-three percent found it unclear and inadequate and felt it was seldom strictly adhered to. There was general agreement that the process needed to be improved, especially because other, unofficial, approaches to seeking approval to establish CHS had emerged.

Mounting pressures to create secondary school places resulted in the MEHRD being inundated with requests from communities, education authorities and members of Parliament to establish their own CHS. The Ministry was pressured to approve 18 CHS in 1996 and a further 24 in 1997. Although the official consultation process was followed in some communities, others simply proceeded to establish their schools and contacted the MEHRD only after the facilities had been completed. Education officials were powerless to stem the tide. In some cases provincial education authorities were bypassed by school communities, which sent formal letters to the MEHRD asking officials to visit, believing this would make the process go faster and eliminate red tape. The closure of most of the seven boarding schools in Guadalcanal during the ethnic unrest exacerbated the pressure as other provinces tried to cater for the displaced students. Senior MEHRD officials interviewed considered that the Ministry needed to take greater control because it simply could not fund all the new schools being built.

The ongoing operation of CHS

The availability and sufficiency of financial and other support for CHS

Once the schools were built and approved, they were eligible to receive central government grants of SI$50,000 per annum for a single-stream school of 35 students per class, or SI$80,000 for a double stream. While no one interviewed knew how the grants were determined, they were to be paid directly into school bank accounts on a quarterly basis. The Government was also responsible for providing teachers and paying their salaries, and for educational materials and textbooks. MEHRD officials believed that a new formula based on unit costs should be developed. Provincial education authorities were not directly responsible for financing CHS, though some (e.g., Isabel province) had tried to assist. However, a provincial politician noted that because of cash flow problems, some CHS did not receive any grants from the province. A church education authority responsible for one of the case study schools did not provide direct cash grants but had helped provide land. It also allowed the school to accept students who had been displaced by the ethnic tensions and who were unable to pay fees. A further source of funding was the constituency development fund from the national member of Parliament, or the ward development fund of the provincial member of Parliament. These are discretionary funds for the members to use as they see fit, so there was no guarantee that a CHS would receive any money from these sources.

There was overwhelming agreement (98 percent) from interviewees that the central government grants were insufficient. Many schools were not even getting the full allocation to which they were entitled: some received less than half, and then only after long delays. The Government struggled to pay the grants because of its cash flow problems. Its ability to pay was also affected by the rapid growth of CHS: the amount budgeted would have been sufficient for the first 50 schools, yet over 90 were built.

Parents made a substantial contribution to resourcing their local schools. All the CHS in the study charged fees to parents in the SI$400–$600 range per annum, as well as other levies for work funds, building funds and uniforms. For example, one school charged a SI$20 fine on parents who failed to turn up for compulsory work scheduled on the first Saturday of the month. Two other schools charged a building fee of SI$100 per child. However, much of the parents' resources were in kind. They provided free labour and building materials such as timber, sand and gravel, and also held fundraising activities within the community. A MEHRD official noted that resources from parents were invaluable: if properly quantified, the community contribution would be greater than that of the Government. It is worth noting here that the two CHS built with direct World Bank assistance, Bishop Epalle and Gizo, cost SI$1.8 million and SI$2 million, respectively.

In retrospect it is amazing that the communities were able to start a CHS almost totally on their own. The Government's grant assistance to CHS only subsidised the tremendous and overwhelming effort given by communities. As one CHS principal asserted:

> This was the parents' initiative and a parents' school. From the beginning, when this school started up to now, it was marvellous. Money came from overseas but it was the manpower from parents that put these buildings up, cleaned the place and all that sort of thing. They were really tremendous.

A provincial official noted that not all communities were able to provide building materials easily. For example, if their atoll produced copra, they could not fell trees for timber so they would have to buy building supplies that occurred naturally elsewhere, thus incurring extra costs. There were other equity issues. While school fees appeared to be the main source of funds, the level of fees varied according to what the school boards deemed acceptable and affordable for their locality. Those in remote rural areas could not charge fees as high as those in urban areas, but many of their costs were similar.

International literature shows that educational decentralisation is an expensive undertaking and requires the provision of adequate financial resources for its successful implementation (Bhindi 1987; Gannicott & McGavin, 1987; Rondinelli, 1981). This fact needs to be taken into account in assessing the establishment CHS. In the period during which the research was undertaken, the establishment and operation of CHS was impeded by financial constraints, long delays in receiving payments and unrealistic levels of central and provincial government grants. Scarce financial resources meant that future developments had to be prioritised and every possible efficiency sought. However, the overwhelming impact of the involvement and contribution from parents and communities in the establishment of CHS has revealed a potential resource not previously realised. The income and expenditure survey carried out in 1999 (World Bank, 2000) provides strong evidence that communities will support their local schools. The explosive growth of CHS is further evidence. Equity concerns must be addressed, but this involvement will continue to be vital.

The administration of CHS

Educational decentralisation normally entails local communities playing a more active role in administration as well as in the resourcing of schools. The research therefore asked questions about school governance and administration to explore whether there were any perceived differences between the new CHS and the more traditional national secondary schools and provincial secondary schools.

Half the interviewees noted that central government continued to carry out its traditional roles of granting approval for establishment; providing grants, teachers, teacher training and salaries; teacher discipline; determining conditions of service; supplying educational materials and equipment; conducting school inspections and examinations; selecting students and monitoring; developing the curriculum; and formulating overall policy and planning for the secondary sector. However, 10 senior officials indicated they would like to see the MEHRD play a facilitating role rather than imposing strict guidelines, which can dampen community enthusiasm and support. In addition, strict guidelines can impose structures that do not take into account unique situations in different parts of the country.

With the exception of Isabel province, where participants felt the provincial education authority had provided adequate assistance, most interviewees, both at the community and central level, felt dissatisfied with provincial support. A principal noted:

There are education authorities that are not actually playing an active role and simply depend on the central government grants and communities. So in a way they are just there as controlling authorities but not actually involved in providing the actual finances, advice and assistance in running.

There were complaints that education authorities did not visit the new schools, did not attend meetings where their professional advice would have been helpful and did not provide any additional resources. There was considerable support for them to play a wider, more decisive role.

The principals of the six case study schools were experienced teachers who had all held other principalships before appointment to their CHS. However, for the four who had supervised the setting up of their schools from scratch, there were considerable new responsibilities. Essentially, they played a pivotal role. They needed to liaise with the MEHRD, their local education authorities, the primary principal, school committee and communities. They had to ensure the site was suitable and that parents and communities understood their roles, they had to supervise construction of classrooms and staff housing and they had to work with the local committee to prepare the school budget and establish bank accounts. They were also required to make regular reports on progress to stakeholders, ranging from the MEHRD to local community members, and encourage fundraising. They estimated that these processes could take from six months to three years.

In addition to working on the physical infrastructure, each principal had a range of professional tasks to ensure their new school was ready to receive pupils. They were involved with their local education authorities in recruiting teachers, ordering textbooks and selecting students. Once staff were appointed, they were involved in developing school policies and procedures for discipline, timetabling and resource use. Once pupils were enrolled, principals were responsible for collecting school fees and including them in the budget. They also generally assumed overall administrative responsibility for the primary school and even the early childhood section. They pointed out that the complexity of the role would be difficult for principals appointed without prior leadership experience and/or training.

Parents and community members had a crucial role to play in determining that a school should be established and in providing land, labour and building materials for its construction. This tended to reinforce their sense of involvement and ownership. Whereas parents whose children attended a provincial secondary school or national secondary school tended to delegate responsibility to teachers and the controlling authorities, the CHS parents needed little encouragement to continue their support for the development of the school. Often they were willing to take on board responsibilities without waiting for the MEHRD or local authorities to advise them, and they wished to be consulted about professional decisions such as the selection of students or appointment of staff. Some participants suggested that because many local education authorities had displayed little interest in the CHS, their legal status as controlling authorities should be withdrawn and the responsibilities transferred to individual communities. They believed this could eliminate confusion and red tape.

However, the research uncovered a number of issues that needed to be resolved to pave the way for a smooth transition to greater local control of CHS. Although it was clear that there was real decentralisation in the establishment of CHS, with the initiative and energy coming from local communities, MEHRD officials suggested that the process should be formalised through the development of memoranda of understanding that clearly outline respective roles and allow for the handing over of more power to lower levels of management, so that they can continue to be involved in their operation and maintenance.

Included in this process should be an understanding of the boundaries between professional and lay decision making. Cases were described where parents' feelings of ownership could be counterproductive: one local authority official noted that if children performed poorly in their Solomon Islands School Certificate (SISC) examination, parents felt they had the right to force the principal to enrol them in the CHS anyway. There were other examples of interference. An official noted:

> In some schools I have been to the chairman even went so far as going into the classroom to check what the teachers are actually doing. I do not blame them because no one tells them where their line of responsibility ends. We urgently need some sort of guidelines in this area concerning management and operation of CHS that we can refer to so that we do not step on each other's toes.

The quality of leadership in CHS overall was also raised as a concern because of the shortage of teachers, the practice of appointing newly graduated secondary trained teachers or appointing the headmaster of the local primary school to head the CHS. Such people lack training in educational leadership and administration, and a number of participants identified inadequate skills in financial, staff and school resource management, conflict resolution and communication. This could be exacerbated by the fact that most provincial education authorities were staffed by former primary teachers, with limited knowledge of secondary systems, and were therefore reluctant to provide advice and support. There could also be tension between the primary and CHS administration on the same site.

Two-thirds of the research participants believed that the management of CHS was frustrated by unclear definitions of roles and responsibilities. A similar number felt that the management of CHS had been frustrated by lack of training for those appointed to their new roles as CHS principals. A range of suggestions to ameliorate this situation included short and longer term courses covering areas such as the basic principles of management, financial management, personnel management and curriculum and resource management. In addition, participants recommended training for school committee members and provincial education officers in monitoring school effectiveness and in governance.

Although the policy to create CHS was apparently unplanned, by the time the research was carried out they had already become a firmly established part of the secondary education system. The data revealed strong desires from politicians, administrators, local officials and community groups to build further CHS so that all children could have access to education till at least the end of Form 3. Participants expressed great disappointment at the MEHRD's move to freeze approval for new schools from 2000 because of the tensions and financial difficulties. Interviews also revealed that some schools tried to expand by "adding tops" to CHS; in other words, adding Forms 4 and 5 rather than providing more places at Forms 1 to 3. As this trend was likely to continue, this raised serious resource implications for the Government and the MEHRD. Most interviewees supported moves to decentralise more CHS functions to lower levels, and there was no support for any recentralisation, which, it was claimed, would kill the CHS movement. However, participants at all levels wanted the Government to provide more resources.

Issues and problems facing CHS

A shortage of qualified teachers—especially in areas such as science, home economics, industrial arts and agriculture—was identified as a major issue. This resulted both in teachers carrying heavy loads with large classes of students, and in teachers being asked to cover subjects of which they had little knowledge. Even if a school had a sufficient number of teachers, they might not reflect the appropriate subject mix. One principal explained that of the three teachers on his staff, one was a maths/business studies teacher and the other two were agriculture teachers, yet between them they were expected to cover all nine subjects in the curriculum. They had to engage a local primary teacher for home economics and the local priest for Bible knowledge. Other schools were unable to offer any classes in certain subjects. MEHRD officials believed that a priority in teacher education should be to upskill primary teachers and provide teaching expertise for those with subject qualifications. Co-ordinated in-service training programmes were seen as being crucial.

CHS also faced shortages of textbooks and equipment. One official offered examples of five pupils sharing a single textbook. The geography and scattered population of the Solomon Islands, which makes distribution difficult, made these shortages worse. The fact that the Curriculum Development Centre produces many curriculum materials locally makes the process cheaper, but reprints are made possible only by external aid. Shortages of warehouse space, unreliable transport and the inability to hire staff to deal with deliveries all added to the frustrations experienced by both schools and officials. Participants also highlighted the fact that communications between Honiara, provincial headquarters and CHS were not dependable. Two principals reported having to travel to provincial headquarters in order to ring Honiara, or to the nearest sub-base to contact provincial headquarters by VHF radio. The situation was improved once the Education Resource Unit in Honiara became fully operational, and would be improved further if proper storage facilities could be built in provincial areas. But transport from Honiara remained a problem. The quality of education in CHS could be handicapped unless logistical support is improved.

In spite of the impressive contribution of local parents and communities, schools identified a lack of proper buildings and facilities, especially for specialist laboratories and workshops. This made practical work difficult, and some schools taught only the theoretical components of subjects. Where science labs were built using local materials, the building often deteriorated quickly and schools experienced difficulty in storing chemicals, equipment and other supplies because of lack of storage, high humidity and lack of electricity. Many CHS did not have halls, libraries, storerooms or staffrooms. Some lacked running water and proper sanitation. These conditions made attracting staff difficult. The researcher (Derek Sikua) believed the implications for the MEHRD were clear: unless it moved quickly to ensure the CHS were well equipped, and placed a sufficient emphasis on practical/vocational skills, the social consequences could be devastating, and might include a massive increase in the drift of unemployed youth to urban areas in search of work.

Accommodation for staff and students was also problematic. A number of CHS were forced to take boarders in order to enrol students from smaller villages, and so needed dormitories and dining facilities. Some schools had to send students home when funds for food supplies were exhausted; others sent students home each weekend to get a week's supply of food. Some students had to be put up by relatives. Several participants noted that these children did not always receive the level of care and supervision they would have received from their parents. Host families might treat students as extra helping hands in the gardens or around the house, which meant it was difficult for them to complete their homework. It was felt that the MEHRD needed to put in place proper facilities to make sure the health and learning environments of the students were not compromised.

Land matters raised further issues. Most of the rural CHS and their associated primary schools are built on land in tribal or customary ownership, which is prone to land disputes. There have been examples of people claiming unrealistic compensation from the Government. In addition, some CHS have insufficient land for expansion, practical plots for agriculture, or sports grounds. In rural areas the local schools may not produce enough students to fill a class of 35, so they need to enrol students from nearby areas, who need to board. Yet space is needed for essential facilities. This pointed to the need for the MEHRD to encourage moves to legally acquire sufficient land for educational purposes.

All these issues were related to the inadequate finance available to the CHS. However, taken together, the issues raised concerns over the quality of education the CHS were able to provide. An MEHRD participant noted:

> To people down there, it look[s] as though we now have three types of secondary school ... My observation is that people think the learning received from NHS is better tha[n] what is received in PHS, and learning received in CHS is third rate.

To what extent have CHS achieved their goals?

CHS have met the major aim of increasing access to secondary education. Between 1995 and 2001 the secondary enrolment rate increased from 26 percent to 69 percent. Most research participants were convinced that the establishment of more CHS would eventually result in the natural progression of all pupils from primary to lower secondary education. One official commented:

> This is the direction we should be heading if we want to increase access into secondary education and achieve basic education of up to nine years for all our children. As a Ministry, we have been trying to do this for a long time but failed. With CHS, the opportunity to do that is here so we have to keep working hard in this direction.

More than half the interviewees believed that CHS also helped increase the number of secondary places for girls, and that gradually this would result in a larger pool of girls entering senior secondary schools and tertiary education.

Two-thirds of the sample felt that CHS have improved disparities in the distribution of secondary places among the provinces. The percentage of secondary students enrolled in CHS varied among the provinces because some had a higher number of places available in national or provincial secondary schools. Smaller and less populated provinces such as Choiseul, Isabel, Central and Makira had made significant progress, while Rennell and Bellona could admit almost all their Standard 6 pupils into their one secondary school. By 2002, statistics showed that the percentage of students in CHS had risen to 59 percent of all secondary enrolments.

CHS have reduced unit costs in secondary education. An MEHRD official noted that although the Government's budgetary allocation for education had not increased over the previous five years, numbers in secondary education had risen significantly. More children were being educated with the same amount of money, or less. Major savings were made because there were no boarding or transport costs involved in attending CHS and parents were happy that the fees charged by CHS were often half those of the boarding schools. The lower costs were particularly important in rural areas, where parents often had little or no income. Whereas some boarding schools were forced to end their academic year early because of lack of funds to buy food for students, the CHS were able to complete the year.

A key aim of those establishing CHS was to encourage greater parental and community participation in secondary schools. Ownership was demonstrated by local people building schools without relying on central or provincial government, or church authorities. Communities that supplied labour and resources took better care of the schools they had built. In contrast, parents of children attending provincial secondary schools had little interest in school affairs, and the communities expected financial reward before undertaking maintenance work. A CHS school treasurer noted that because of the understanding that the school belonged to them, parents were prepared to raise money and assist in improving facilities. And because the school was located close to the community it became part and parcel of community life:

> When we rely too much on the Government, things move slowly; for example, in boarding schools, which are located far away from communities. For CHS, when we put the responsibilities on the parents, they really work hard and you can see the difference now.

A CHS principal claimed that the strong community support for his school also had a positive influence on the attitude and commitment of his teachers. He believed they were more vigilant and accountable than those with whom he had worked as a provincial secondary school principal. Because many of the CHS were established on top of local primary schools, the community support often spilled over into the primary area as well. In addition, primary and secondary teachers were able to collaborate and share resources.

Proponents of CHS had initially claimed that the new schools would be better placed to enhance the teaching and learning of the local culture and language. There was insufficient evidence, when the interviews were held, to determine whether local language and culture were being integrated into school curricula but participants in the study provided a number of examples of schools assisting the community. An agriculture teacher from a CHS in Western province reported that he conducted a vegetable gardening course for local women in 1999. A teacher from Guadalcanal said that his school and board had agreed to use the school facilities to conduct vocational training for the local community, offering practical courses in mechanics, woodwork, agriculture, fishing techniques, simple bookkeeping, home economics and literacy. However, the researcher found no evidence of schools making use of knowledgeable people from the community.

The relevance of the traditional curriculum was widely questioned, however. Research participants expressed concerns about the mainly academic curriculum offered in CHS, particularly for those whose education was likely to end at Form 3, with few prospects for either employment or further study. One commented:

The secondary education system should be equally geared towards practical/vocational education for self-employment and not only academic education for paid employment and further education. Therefore, the CHS curriculum should provide an avenue for the majority of students to create their own employment, as paid employment is becoming scarce.

Other concerns expressed included the need to ensure input into the curriculum from local culture, knowledge and skills, and the importance of helping students develop leadership, good citizenship and habits of co-operation. Policy makers face the challenges of developing a well balanced "mixed mode" curriculum, allowing for the inclusion of vocational/technical skills and traditional cultures as well as academic skills leading to further education and employment.

Perhaps the strongest endorsement of the community support for the new schools came from a CHS board chairman from Guadalcanal province, who reported that his school remained open during the ethnic conflict in 1999 and 2000. A nearby provincial secondary school and CHS built with World Bank funding, on the other hand, had been forced to close, because of their heterogeneous population and their location away from the students' communities. The World Bank-funded CHS remained closed because it was looted and damaged by militants. The support for CHS is in line with Williams' point that "people value services more highly and take a stronger interest in the nature of the services when they directly contribute finance or labour, however small in amount" (as cited in Bray, 1987, p. 7).

Conclusions

The findings of this study support the view that decentralisation is an appropriate model for Solomon Islands secondary education and that it increases access, female participation and provincial equity, reduces unit costs and encourages community partnership in education. As such, the study makes a valuable contribution to the international literature on educational decentralisation as a key aspect of educational restructuring (Ball, 1990; Fiske, 1996; Govinda, 1997; Levin, 1998).

Decentralisation is claimed to be a means to increase popular participation in education (Fiske, 1996; Nanau, 1995). This study highlighted the fact that community participation and partnership were at the core of the success of CHS. Local people were given the opportunity to actively participate and make development decisions in their own areas, while focusing on nationwide policies (Ocampo, 1991). Decentralisation is also claimed to result in greater efficiency and reduced costs (Nanau, 1995; Fiske, 1996). The costs of CHS are up to three times lower than those of provincial secondary schools and national secondary schools, and benefits of these lower costs were passed on to parents in the form of lower tuition fees.

However, the ongoing success of a decentralised policy such as that adopted by the Solomon Islands Government in developing CHS depends on the quality of its implementation. The study found that five criteria are necessary for sustainable development in a developing country:
- a clear understanding—by all parties concerned—of the purpose and method of decentralisation through the development of a memorandum of understanding
- the provision of adequate resources (teachers, finance and educational materials)
- management structures and procedures that support the overall aim behind educational decentralisation and provide training for leaders and administrators at all levels
- ensuring the structure of the education system and the curriculum are relevant and support the teaching and learning of local cultures and languages, as well as vocational skills for self-employment
- periodic reviews of progress to check problems and align policies.

In the Solomon Islands, decentralisation of secondary education has the support and goodwill of the majority of professionals and laypeople. Nevertheless, there are problems with implementation that need to be overcome. Decentralisation made many demands on government services, available resources and skilled labour. The weaknesses revealed were largely in the structure of the system and the initial professional expertise of the administrators. These weaknesses could be overcome by a clear understanding of the theoretical issues involved, enthusiastic leadership, appropriate professional training programmes, efficient management of resources and systematic restructuring.

References

Ball, S. (1990). *Politics and policy making in education: Explorations in policy sociology*. London and New York: Routledge.

Bhindi, N. (1987). *Decentralisation of education in Solomon Islands and the role of provincial education officers*. Unpublished doctoral thesis, the University of Queensland, Brisbane.

Bray, M. (1987). *New resources for education: Community management and financing of schools*. London: The Commonwealth Secretariat.

Doyle, K. (1983). *Report of the Ministry of Education, Training and Cultural Affairs of the Solomon Islands Government on the organisation structure of the Ministry, division of responsibilities between the Ministry and the provinces, and training needs of senior administrators*. Unpublished report for the World Bank, Solomon Islands Primary Education Project, Ministry of Education, Honiara.

Fiske, E. (1996). *Decentralisation of education: Politics and consensus: Directions in development*. Washington: World Bank.

Gannicott, K., & McGavin, P. (1987). *Solomon Islands financing of education study: Resource and management of primary and secondary schooling in the Solomon Islands: A draft report to the Ministry of Education and Training of the Solomon Islands*. Campbell, ACT: Air Force Defence Force Academy, Centre for Studies in Management and Logistics, University College, the University of New South Wales.

Govinda, R. (1997). *Decentralisation of educational management: Experiences from South Asia*. Paris: UNESCO.

Habu, M. (1983). *The structure of education in the Solomon Islands*. Unpublished paper for the Institute of Education, University of the South Pacific, Fiji.

Levin, B. (1998). An epidemic of education policy: What can we learn from each other? *Comparative Education, 34*(2), 131–142.

Nanau, G. (1995). *Decentralisation, development and popular participation in the Solomon Islands: A study of the provincial government system*. Unpublished master's thesis, University of the South Pacific, Fiji.

Ocampo, R. (1991). Decentralisation and local autonomy: A framework for assessing progress. *Philippines Journal of Public Administration, XXXV*(3), 191–294.

Rondinelli, D. (1981). Government decentralisation in comparative perspective: Theory and practice in developing countries. *International Review of Administrative Sciences, 2*, 133–145.

Thomas, A. (1983). *A review of the Diploma in Administration (Education), University of the South Pacific, and an analysis of the training needs of education administrators in the Solomon Islands*. Armidale, NSW: University of New England, Centre for Administration and Higher Education Studies.

World Bank. (1993). *Staff appraisal report: Solomon Islands third education and training project*. Washington: Population and Human Resources Operations Division, Country Development III, East Asia and Pacific Region.

World Bank. (2000). *Solomon Islands primary and secondary education: A community standard for school financing*. Washington: Human Development Sector Unit, East Asia and the Pacific Region.

Derek Sikua

Derek was born in Ngalitavethi Village, East Tasiboko, Guadalcanal Province. He was educated at Maravovo Senior Primary School and Selwyn College. He completed a Dip. Ed at the University of the South Pacific and a Bachelor of Education at the University of Southern Queensland. Between 1982 and 1986 he worked as a teacher and Deputy Principal at Pawa Secondary School and Waimapuru National Secondary School, then joined the Ministry of Education and Human Resource Development, where he held a number of posts, becoming Permanent Secretary in 1994. He completed a doctorate at the University of Waikato in 2002. He was elected to the national Parliament of the Solomon Islands for the

North East Guadalcanal constituency in 2006 and served as Minister of Education before becoming Prime Minister in November 2007. He is married with five children and lists his interests as reading, writing, sport, bush walking and travel.

Noeline Alcorn

Noeline is an Emeritus Professor of Education at the University of Waikato. She was Dean of the School of Education from 1992-2006 and has been associated with the partnership from the beginning. Her publications are mainly in history and policy studies in education. She has supervised many student theses, including co-supervising that of Derek Sikua.

CHAPTER 2
The Educational and Career Aspirations Solomon Islands' Parents Hold for Their Children

Rose Beuka
Woodford International School, Honiara, Solomon Islands

Jane Strachan
University of Waikato, Hamilton, New Zealand

Introduction

No previous research has explored whether the formal education provided in the Solomon Islands is what parents want for their children. The curriculum in use (particularly at the secondary level) was designed before independence, and though curriculum changes are occurring, it will be some time before they are fully implemented. This suggests that the curriculum may be out of date and unsuitable for preparing students for careers. To explore this idea, research was undertaken to address the following question: What are parents' educational and career aspirations for their children, and what are their (the parents') perceptions of the formal secondary education in the Solomon Islands with respect to their children's preparation for meeting these aspirations?

Secondary education in the Solomon Islands

There are three types of secondary schools in the Solomon Islands: national secondary schools (NSS), provincial secondary schools (PSS) and community high schools (CHS). The NSS are either directly controlled by the central government (two schools) or by different church education authorities (seven schools). Historically, these schools, with one exception (Waimapuru NSS), are some of the oldest established schools in the country. The NSS normally take in the most academically able students nationwide. They offer full, academic secondary courses up to Form 5. With the growing demand for higher secondary education (Forms 6 and 7), most of the NSS are now offering Pacific Senior School Certificate (PSSC) and a University Foundation year. In some instances (Su'u NSS, for example), junior forms (Forms 1–3) have been removed and these schools cater only for the senior forms (Forms 4–7).

The PSS are controlled by provincial educational authorities and were introduced in response to a major review of the education system in 1973. The PSS focus more on a rural, vocationally oriented secondary curriculum, which encourages the development of skills for self-employment (Sikua, 2002). In response to some parents' preference for academic subjects, the PSS have slowly introduced academic subjects alongside vocational subjects, and thereby created the opportunity for PSS students to come back into the academic stream after sitting the Form 4 Entrance Examination (Liligeto, 2001). Currently, all the PSS are now offering the same academic courses as the NSS, and some have added Forms 5, 6 and 7, such as in Honiara High School. This is a major change, because PSS used to offer secondary education only up to Form 3 (Liligeto, 2001). This broadening of secondary education through the PSS caters for more children to be enrolled in the academic stream of secondary education.

The introduction of CHS in 1995 resulted from international comment on the Solomon Islands' highly competitive pyramidal education system that, according to the World Bank (1993, as cited in Sikua, 2002), had so few places that intending students were continually pushed out. As a consequence, since the Solomon Islands Secondary Entrance Examination (SISEE) was introduced, there has been no time in the country's history that all primary school children have gained direct entry into secondary education. In 1994 only 26 percent of primary education students who sat the SISEE progressed on to secondary education.

The high population growth, coupled with the Government's lack of capacity to fund new secondary education, prompted the planning sector of the Ministry of Education and Human Resources Development (MEHRD) to plan to initiate an expansion of quality education, for which community support and initiative were expected. The initiative sparked a huge interest in different communities nationwide. In 1995, nine CHS were opened, but by 2002, 93 CHS were operating either as separate schools or as part of an existing primary school. By 2009 the percentage of primary students progressing to secondary school after sitting the SISEE had increased to 94.8 percent (MEHRD, 2009), a direct result of the establishment of CHS.

Parents' perceptions of education

Parents will always have different perceptions of education, different career aspirations for their children and different views of the school in relation to preparing children for careers. In the Solomon Islands, formal education is considered important and necessary, and a way to gain social and economic advancement.

One of the perceptions parents have of education is that it is a form of investment. According to Sikua (2002), Solomon Islands parents send their children to school in the hope that through a formal education, and especially a formal qualification, children will be able to secure a well paid job and be able to support the family.

Education is therefore seen as a vehicle for getting better pay. This is partly the reason for parents prioritising boys' education over girls' education. The Solomon Islands is mostly a patriarchal society (Bennett, 1987), so investing in girls is often seen as merely investing in the groom's family.

Another perception parents have in relation to education is that it is a means of preparing children for the future (Chomsky, 1988) in a society where people have high expectations, education is seen as the key to success. Parents' perception of education as preparation for work and as preparation for the future are related (Willis, 1980). However, education as preparation for the future is related to how one will "apply" knowledge for a "worthwhile form of life" (Corson, 1988, p. 89). Education as preparation for work and the workplace, on the other hand, is perceived in relation to how education/schooling prepares students directly for the workplace and the type of work they will do (Corson, 1988; Wringe, 1988).

Although education as a preparation for work and the workplace is commonly associated with imparting knowledge and skills to function effectively at work (Corson, 1988; Wringe, 1988), Corson also sees education as enabling students to gain an understanding of, commitment to and efficiency at work. This means that education is about equipping students not only with practical skills and knowledge but also with the right attitudes to work and the workplace.

Parents' educational and career aspirations for their children

Parents undoubtedly send their children to formal education with set intentions, although, in countries other than Solomon Islands the intentions may not always be educational and/or career related (Best, 1980).

The relationship between education and employment can be a major influence in sending children to school, and this relationship can be reflected in the way parents affect their children's choice of career. This is not only indirectly through family demographics, such as family size and income (Boatwright, Ching, & Parr, 1992; Penick & Jepsen, 1992) but, more importantly, through how families interact with each other (Trusty & Watts, 1996).

One indicator that parents have educational career aspirations for their children is reflected in the similarities between the adolescents' and parents' values in relation to their parents' occupation (Lapan, Hinekeman, Adams, & Turner, 1999). Parents often aspire for their children to pursue careers or occupations related to the parents' interest and occupation (Boatwright et al., 1992; Eccles, 1994; Mau & Bikos, 2000). However, there are also parents who want their children to pursue careers or professions that are different from their own. When parents place high expectations on their children, the children often respond accordingly, and in this way students can pursue careers outside their parents' occupation while fulfilling their parents' academic or vocational expectations for them (Turner & Lapan, 2002). In the situation where parents have other occupational expectations for their children (beyond the parents' occupations, for instance), these career expectations can filter down to their children's career decisions (Peterson, Stivers, & Peters, 1986).

Culture also influences career aspirations. In the Solomon Islands, for instance, because of the patriarchal "big man" system (Keesing, 1978), it is common for some cultural groups to see some jobs as specifically for men or for women. Although there have been some recent changes in cultural practices, as shown by women being involved in jobs that used to be solely for men, generally women are still not expected to be trained as mechanics or carpenters, or to work on ships. Men, likewise, are not expected to be home economics or early childhood teachers. These traditional sex-role stereotypes are powerful influences (Strachan, Akao, Kilavanwa & Warsal, 2010).

The research design

The research described in this article used a qualitative, constructivist research methodology. The constructivist paradigm is one that values each individual perception and recognises that there is more than one interpretation of the same data, and of reality (Guba & Lincoln, 1998). This means there are "multiple constructed realities" (Krauss, 2005, p. 759). The constructivist paradigm thus recognises individual views based on individual experiences and perceptions.

The choice of this kind of paradigm was further consolidated by a goal of the research project to explore parents' own educational and career aspirations for their children and their perception of the secondary education system in the Solomon Islands in relation to preparing students for future careers. Constructivist research sees data collection as a discovery process (Krauss, 2005) that allows the researcher to take the point of view of the participants through an interactive interview.

Semistructured interviewing was used to collect information from the eight parents. This method was considered the most appropriate one for this study because it is a means of collecting data that "permits flexibility" (Burns, 2000, p. 424), and it involves a social and free-flowing conversation between the researcher and the participant (Burns, 2000; Cohen, Manion, & Morrison, 2000). Semistructured interviewing was also particularly relevant for the context of this research because of the oral tradition of the Solomon Islands.

The eight parents in this study were interviewed in their homes. The language used in the interview sessions with all participants was pidgin English, the *lingua franca* of the Solomon Islands. The choice of pidgin English as the language of interview was significant, because all participants understood and communicated comfortably in this language.

The findings

The findings are organised using the following categories: parents' educational and career aspirations for their children; parents' understanding of the Solomon Islands education system; and parents' views of vocational schools.

Parents' educational and career aspirations for their children

The careers specifically mentioned by parents were teaching, nursing, office/administration, accounting, doctor, pilot and a career related to agriculture. A probable reason for parents specifying these careers is that, in the Solomon Islands, medical doctors and graduates with teaching or nursing qualifications have always been able to get a job.

As we saw, some parents wanted their children to pursue careers other than those in which they were involved. Parents who did not have secondary education, for instance, wanted their children to get a secondary education and subsequently get a well paid job compared to their own job. However, some parents with secondary or higher education and with well paid jobs still wanted their children to get different jobs from what they were doing. One educated parent with a well paid job stated, "I do not want my children to take up the career [I am doing] anymore, other careers yes, they can go for it" (M1).

Some parents did not want their children to pursue their careers because of their experiences in those jobs and because they did not want to deprive their children of other opportunities. Other parents had career aspirations for their children but would rather respect any career choice and decision their children made based on the children's interests. One parent commented:

> I have some careers in mind. However, I cannot force my children to take up those careers. Children have interests in other careers too, besides those I have in mind. So because of this, I will leave it up to them to make their choice. (M3)

Some parents genuinely felt that children should make their own career choices, with support from parents, because the children needed job satisfaction and enjoyment in the careers they pursued. Also, some parents were not as educated as their children, and hence felt that the children's choice would be an educated one.

Finally, some parents had careers in mind for their children but were reluctant to be specific with the researcher because they saw her on a personal level (someone who knew them) rather than in a professional capacity as a researcher. For instance, when parent M3 was asked if he could be specific about the career he had in mind, the response was, "I do not want to be embarrassed around you if you know that my children did not achieve what I aspire for them".

The fact that parents' aspirations differed is replicated in the international literature and is not unique to the Solomon Islands. However, the Solomon Islands' context is unique, and does influence the particular career aspirations parents have for their children.

Influences on parents' career aspirations for their children

The influence of better pay and future financial security was a dominant factor in parents' career aspirations for their children: basically, parents wanted their children's future career to be well paid. This could account for some parents wanting their children to pursue careers where they could earn a living from self-employment. However, the findings of this study suggest that better pay and future financial security were mostly associated with academic careers rather than vocational careers. For example, one parent stated:

> I want my children to be educated and have a well-paid job so that they can be self-reliant. At school they learn knowledge that might be helpful for their future. As a parent, I see education as the only way for a better living in the future for our children. (F4)

In the context of the Solomon Islands, the type of job he/she does defines a person. Parents aspired for their children to have academic-related careers where they could be looked at with envy by others.

Parents were also influenced by the usefulness and appropriateness of a career in urban and rural situations. They wanted their children to undertake certain careers on the understanding that the children could have their careers in either urban or rural areas—including a regular salary. For example, careers in an agricultural area were seen as useful because, with knowledge, a person can make better use of customary land to maximise the yield. And a career in teaching or in nursing can be found in both urban and rural areas. In contrast, a computer expert cannot find employment and a regular income when retiring to the rural villages. The following comment illustrates this view: "I want them [children] to take up a career in teaching and nursing because they can still be teachers or nurses even if they go back to the village" (F2). This belief has been reinforced by the ethnic conflict in the Solomon Islands. During this time (2002), people who were employed in the private sector in professions such as computing and accounting were deeply affected. When they escaped from the town there were no jobs for them in the rural villages.

Parents' career aspirations for their children were also influenced by what they perceived would be to the advantage of their children in the near future, particularly in a context where job opportunities with good pay are scarce in the Solomon Islands. Such an influence was evident more among those parents who were conscious of the economic activities going on around them and who read newspapers to update themselves on the likely future trends in employment:

> … [work in the] mines, I heard rumors that our customary land has minerals under it. I think that it's good that one of my children is trained in this area while the mineral is still to be confirmed and no prospecting has been done yet. When the development eventuates, we already have someone who is qualified in the area. (M2)

Some parents thought that it was important not to neglect cultural values when pursuing a career. Although financial rewards were seen as important, they did not want to break the cultural norms of their community or society: "there are jobs that fit only boys or girls" (F2). Such comments are not new, especially from parents of the older generation or who are still very much part of their cultural traditions. Cultural stereotyping of jobs is a very strong influence on the type of careers they aspire to for their children. For instance, girls are not expected to do carpentry because it involves climbing up houses, which is strictly forbidden for girls.

Secondary education preparation of children for future careers

Some parents did not think that the school alone should be responsible for preparing their children for future careers; the preparation should be a joint effort between the schools and the parents:

> As parents we should not depend entirely on the school but we should also actively educate our children at home because that is their first place to learn ... the school only provides general knowledge. As parents, we should help our children with their subjects to try to help them choose the subjects that will help to gear them towards the type of career you want for them. (F4)

However, comment was also made that secondary education provides the foundations that are important not only for careers immediately after secondary education but also for going on to further higher educational institutions. For example:

> Schools are important because they provide some guidance to children and equip them for different jobs. Before you work, you must know how to read, write and to do other things both mentally and physically. When children go on to further education, they would also then gain some more knowledge that will help guide and equip them towards the job they would do. (F1)

The influence of individual teachers, as well as the subjects that were taught at school, was mentioned:

> It depends on the teachers. Some simply do their job because of the fortnightly salary they receive. They do not really have a passion for the kids they teach. For these types of teachers, their students might

end up not pursuing any career or getting a job after completing the school years ... The subjects will help guide the student towards the career he/she wants. (M3)

Some parents considered that the children were so busy with academic work or with other immediate activities and issues that they did not often reflect on the type of career they might want to pursue. When asked about this, one parent responded:

... sometimes children did not think about their career or set their aim when they were at school. They go to school just for the sake of schooling or just want to complete the year. I think most children did not think about career planning. Although parents might have aims or plans for their children, they [children] sometimes did not achieve the aims and plans. (M4)

With the introduction and establishment of CHS (see also Chapter 1), the rate of students being pushed out of the education system at the primary education level in the Solomon Islands has dramatically reduced. Some of the CHS have introduced senior secondary forms (Forms 4–5), which means increased numbers of students with Form 5 Secondary School Certificate. However, the rate at which these students get employment is not high. More and more secondary graduated students are without any form of employment. Unless they get further specific job training they might not be able to employ themselves:

... children leaving school from these levels [Forms 3 to 7] did not get jobs. Most of them just roam the streets. Even if we want them to do some kind of job, they do not meet the required standards and are just wasting their time as well as their parents' money on school fees. (F1)

When parents were asked how they expected the school to prepare children for careers, the responses indicated a desire for including all curriculum subjects in schools and the recruitment of specialised, well qualified teachers in all subjects. This is an issue in most of the Solomon Islands secondary schools because of the shortage of teachers and a lack of facilities and resources. There are schools that do not offer science or practical subjects (such as home economics or industrial arts) because of the shortage of resources, including qualified teachers. Most teachers who teach up to Form 5 are diploma-level graduates of the School of Education at the Solomon Islands College of Higher Education. This programme was designed to train teachers for junior secondary education levels only (Forms 1–3):

> As a parent, I would like to see that the schools offer all curriculum subjects that should be offered at the secondary level. This is to expose students to the bigger picture of the opportunities available out in the world related to the subjects. It is also important that these subjects are taught by teachers who are specialised not only in the theoretical aspect of the subjects but practical as well. (M2)

Parents' understanding of the Solomon Islands education system

Parents' understanding of what is taught in secondary schools was related more to the core examinable subjects, especially English and mathematics. Only one parent also included Christian education and science, and another parent included social science and science.

The parents' level of understanding of the curriculum may have two implications. One is that the content of curriculum subjects is not a topic of discussion; a subject is simply considered to be important because it is one of the subjects necessary for progression to the next level in the education system. The other implication is that parents who do not know the content of the curriculum may not be able to say conclusively whether the curriculum is either helping or not helping career development: "I am not really sure of what is taught in the classroom but the main subjects we know about are mathematics, English, Christian education and science" (F3).

When the parents were asked to explain how they thought what was taught at the secondary level was or was not helping to prepare their children to meet their career aspirations for them, the responses indicated two themes. First, some parents viewed secondary education positively and were generally happy with the academic focus, particularly for enabling children to improve their mathematical knowledge, reading and writing ability and creativity. These were considered to be important because they could be used by the student when called upon in different areas. One parent, for instance, commented that "some of the subjects taught at the examinable levels seem alright to me. For instance, mathematics helps in preparing children for accounting type jobs" (M3). The positive comments about the academic focus of the curriculum reflect the value placed on academic education rather than on vocational education.

Second, some parents considered that, although the secondary education curriculum and the schools were trying their best to help the children, what was offered was not enough to meet the varied nature of the workplace. For instance, one parent stated:

> The emphasis on the four core subjects [English, mathematics, science and social science] is good. However, they do not really sufficiently equip children to meet the high demand of the workplace. When children are pushed out of the education system, I do not think they will be able to do any good at all with the knowledge gained. I would say it only prepares students for [the] academic stream but not for work. (M2)

This argument is significant in the Solomon Islands' context because it is not only unrealistic for *all* students to pursue academically related careers, but opportunities for *any* students to pursue careers in the academic stream are very limited. Currently, the practical subjects, which are also known as "optional" subjects (if offered in schools), are allocated fewer teaching hours per week compared to the academic subjects. Previously they were not even considered an important subject in the selection process to get a place in Form 6. This indicates that academic subjects are now valued more highly than vocational subjects.

Parents' views of vocational education

Parents tended to associate vocational education and/or vocational schools as institutions where the method of knowledge and skill acquisition was more related to the traditional ways of learning, in which students learnt by doing. However, even though parents thought that vocational education prepared students for life, it was felt that students with vocational training should be given the opportunity to go to higher technical institutions. For instance, one parent stated:

> It would be good if vocational schools improve to another higher level so that when children finish from there, they can move on further through higher vocational schools. (M2)

This is a concern for many potential vocational students. Currently, students who get vocational qualifications have a very limited number of scholarships available to them. At the School of Industrial Development at the Solomon Islands College of Higher Education, almost all students are self-sponsored. This effectively eliminates many from having the opportunity to apply for entry, because they would not be able to afford the fees. However, parents valued the practical skills learnt in the vocational schools because they are useful in helping school leavers to find paid employment. A parent stated:

> The good thing about vocational schools is that children learn a particular skill. And so when they leave school, they have more chances of going straight into the job type in which they acquired their skills.

Some parents preferred a balance between academic and practical learning, yet when asked to choose which they would prefer for their own children, all parents preferred the formal secondary education system (academic). This preference was influenced by the career aspirations they had for their children, as high aspirations were more likely to lead to financial security:

> As a parent, I prefer formal secondary education. This is because if the [children] go to the vocational stream, they might not get into the career I aspire for them. (F4)

Some concluding thoughts

Few research studies have been undertaken by a Solomon Islander on Solomon Islands education. In the developing world, where there is little documented research, it is difficult to find contextualised scholarship. This study can be used as a reference for future educators and researchers not only for the Solomon Islands' context but internationally as well. The findings presented here have implications for education stakeholders everywhere. In particular, teachers, curriculum developers and education policy makers need to consider parents' view and expectations of the education system, as noted by Liligeto (2001, p. 6): "[they] need concrete evidence of what people view as being appropriate for their citizens". The Solomon Islands' secondary curriculum needs to reflect the changes that are taking place, both locally and internationally, in education and employment so that it provides children with skills that employers (the job market) require of secondary education. Conversely, employers need to clearly define the skills and qualities they are looking for in students.

The findings also suggest that secondary schools need to offer the full range of curriculum subjects to give students a wider scope of career possibilities. This has resource implications, because it would mean that all schools would need to be resourced with teachers, facilities and teaching materials that enhance the teaching of all subjects. It could be helpful in preparing young people for work if the secondary education curriculum includes life and work skills in an organised way, either directly as part of compulsory subjects or as a stand-alone curriculum subject. However, this is a big ask in the current economic climate. The Solomon Islands Government, like other governments worldwide, is experiencing a recession. Money to fund education in the Solomon Islands has never been plentiful, and it is even less so now.

This study indicates that some parents do not really know what their children are being taught. Secondary schools could play a role here: informing parents about the curriculum content taught in secondary schools could help parents to help their children make informed life, study, career and employment decisions. There are very limited academic career opportunities for students, yet the secondary education system is emphasising academic subjects over vocational and technical subjects. The MEHRD could part-sponsor more students to pursue specific vocational and technical education, just as it does for teachers and nurses. Which vocations are prioritised will need to align with the country's workforce needs.

With the increase in secondary education places for students, and changes in the work environment, parents' perceptions of the secondary education system are important. Even if the economy cannot cope with the demand for employment, parents will always be the first point of contact for their children. The reality is that the vast majority of young people leaving school in the Solomon Islands will not go on to further study or paid employment. They will live their lives in the rural villages. Parents need to know that the secondary education system has equipped their children to function effectively in paid employment *or* in village life.

References

Bennett, J. A. (1987). *Wealth of the Solomons: A history of a Pacific archipelago, 1800–1978*. Honolulu: Hawaii University Press.

Best, F. (1980). The time of our lives: The parameters of lifetime distribution of education, work and leisure. In S. Reedy & M. Woodhead (Eds.), *Contemporary issues in education: Family, work and education* (pp. 380– 392). London: Hodder and Stoughton.

Boatwright, M. A., Ching, M., & Parr, A. (1992). Factors that influence students' decision to attain college. *Journal of Instructional Psychology, 19*, 79–86.

Burns, R. B. (2000). *Introduction to research methods* (4th ed.). Melbourne: Longman.

Chomsky, N. (1988). Towards a humanistic conception of education and work. In D. Corson (Ed.), *Education for work: Background to policy and curriculum* (pp. 19–32). Palmerston North: Dunmore Press.

Cohen, L., Manion, L., & Morrison, K. (2000). *Research methods in education* (5th ed.). New York: Routledge Falmer.

Corson, D. (1988). *Education for work: Background to policy and curriculum*. Palmerston North: Dunmore Press.

Eccles, J. S. (1994). Understanding women's educational and occupational choices. *Psychology of Women Quarterly, 18*, 585–609.

Guba, E. G., & Lincoln, Y. S. (1998). Competing paradigms in qualitative research. In N. K. Denzin & Y. S. Lincoln (Eds.), *The landscape of qualitative research* (pp. 195–220). Thousand Oaks, CA: Sage.

Keesing, R. M. (1978). *Elota's story: The life and times of a Solomon Island Big Man*. Brisbane: University of Queensland Press.

Krauss, S. E. (2005). Research paradigms and meaning making: A primer. *The Qualitative Report, 10*(4), 758–770. Retrieved 18 November 2007, from http://www.novaedu/ssss/QR/QR10-4/krauss.pdf

Lapan, R. T., Hinkeman, J. M., Adams, A., & Turner, S. (1999). Understanding rural adolescents' interests, values and efficacy expectations. *Journal of Career Development, 26*(2), 107–124.

Liligeto, A. G. (2001). *Perceptions of technology and technology education in Fiji and the Solomon Islands*. Unpublished doctoral thesis, University of Waikato, Hamilton.

Mau, W. C., & Bikos, L. H. (2000). Educational and vocation aspirations of minority and female students: A longitudinal study. *Professional School Counseling, 2*, 161–166.

MEHRD. (2009). *Performance Assessment Framework, 2006–2008*. Honiara: Author.

Penick, N. I., & Jepsen, D. A. (1992). Family functioning and adolescence career development. *Career Development Quarterly, 40*(3), 208–222.

Peterson, G. W., Stivers, M. E., & Peters, D. F. (1986). Family versus nonfamily: Significant others for the career decisions of low-income youth. *Family Relations, 35*, 417–424.

Richard, A., & Friesen, J. D. (1992). The intentions of parents in influencing the career development of their children. *Career Development Quarterly, 40*(3), 198–207.

Sikua, D. D. (2002). *The decentralization of education in a developing country: The case of community high schools in Solomon Islands*. Unpublished doctoral thesis, University of Waikato, Hamilton.

Strachan, J., Akao, S., Kilavanwa, B., & Warsal, D. (2010). You have to be a servant to all: Melanesian women's educational leadership experiences. *School Leadership and Management, 30*(1), 65–76.

Trusty, J., & Watts, R. E. (1996). Parents' perceptions of career information resources. *Career Development Quarterly, 44*(3), 242.

Turner, S., & Lapan, R. T. (2002). Perceptions of parent support in adolescents' career development. *Career Development Quarterly, 50*(3), 1–3.

Willis, P. (1980). Education and qualifications. In S. Reedy & M. Woodhead (Eds.), *Contemporary issues in education: Family, work and education* (pp. 91–96). London: Hodder and Stoughton.

Wringe, W. (1988). Education, schooling and the world of work. In D. Corson (Ed.), *Education for work: Background to policy and curriculum* (pp. 33–46). Palmerston North: Dunmore Press.

Rose Beuka

Rose is from the island of Malaita. She did her primary teacher education in the Solomon Islands, her bachelor's degree in education at USP and her Master of Education at the University of Waikato. She is currently working as a learning support teacher of maths and English at Woodford International School in Honiara. Rose is married with three children, two girls and a boy and is a keen spectator of soccer and tennis.

Jane Strachan

Jane is an Associate Professor in Education at the University of Waikato. She has been director of the partnership between the Faculty of Education at Waikato and the School of Education, SICHE, since its inception in 2006. She has worked as a volunteer in Vanuatu and has a commitment to gender equity and the leadership of women. She has published widely and supervised the theses of a number of Pacific students, including Rose Beuka.

CHAPTER 3

Mi Wanfala Tisa Nao, Bata!: Beginning Secondary Teachers' Professional Learning in the Solomon Islands

Patricia Rodie
Doctoral student, University of Waikato, Hamilton, New Zealand

Introduction

As a secondary teacher educator at the School of Education, Solomon Islands College of Higher Education (SICHE) for more than 12 years, and head of school for three years, I have had a lengthy involvement in the development of teacher education programmes and the preparation of secondary teachers for Solomon Islands secondary schools. I initiated a review and redevelopment of the teacher education programmes at the School of Education in 2005. I have participated in deliberations about the quality of teachers and teacher education programmes. I was also involved in the Solomon Islands Education Sector Investment and Reform Programme (ESIRP), which set out to identify issues in various sectors of the education system, including teacher education. These experiences led me to pursue research on teacher education and professional development in the Solomon Islands' context.

My broad research interest covers teacher education and professional development, from the preservice phase through to the early years of teaching. The aim of my current study was to find out how prepared secondary teacher graduates from the School of Education felt at the end of their teacher education programmes, the kind of professional support they need as beginning teachers and whether Solomon Islands secondary schools have adequate professional support systems in place to promote early career learning and development. My study was guided by the overarching question: What are the self-perceptions of beginning secondary teachers about their preparedness to teach, and their induction and professional learning experiences during the first two years of their teaching careers in the Solomon Islands' context? Answers to this question could contribute to improving current teacher education and professional development practices in the Solomon Islands by informing policy decisions that will bring about positive change.

Context

The School of Education has been the sole provider of initial teacher education for the formal education sector in the Solomon Islands over the past two decades. Since its inception in 1988 it has been mandated to prepare teachers by providing teacher education programmes through both preservice and inservice modes. However, the School of Education has focused on preservice teacher education.

The School of Education's mission statement (1998) stipulates that its role is to prepare teachers who are of "quality, well educated to teach in today's Solomon Islands, provide relevant education for all Solomon Islanders, and are aware of their important roles as agents of change for a better Solomon Islands" (SICHE, 1998, p. 11).

The School of Education endeavours to help preservice teachers develop professional attitudes, values, knowledge and skills, guided by its underlying principle: to educate quality teachers for Solomon Islands schools. Between 1988 and 2008 the school has offered a range of teacher education programmes. It has educated and graduated more than 5,000 teachers, who are currently serving in schools throughout the nine provinces in the Solomon Islands. However, little research has been conducted to explore the level of preparedness of the teachers who have graduated from its teacher education programmes.

The teacher education reviews conducted between 2004 and 2005 (Taylor & Pollard, 2004; Wrightson, 2005) revealed a number of issues relating to teachers' performance, professional behaviour and conditions of service. These issues included staff and student absenteeism, lack of commitment and motivation, lack of in-depth knowledge of subject content and unprofessional behaviour. The reviews also reported a lack of formal induction programmes for beginning teachers, lack of professional development and in-service education programmes for teachers, delayed registration of probationers and generally poor conditions of service. Some of these issues might already have been addressed, but I believe that others remain.

Currently, the School of Education's responsibility for preservice teacher education extends as far as the end of the teacher education programmes it offers. The responsibility for providing professional support for new teacher graduates rests with relevant departments at the Ministry of Education and Human Resources Development (MEHRD), the education authorities and school management. However, when this study was conducted, it seemed there was a lack of co-ordinated induction and professional development programmes for beginning teachers in secondary schools.

Method

In this study I took an interpretive qualitative research approach in order to get in-depth insights into the self-perceptions and professional learning experiences of a cohort of beginning secondary teachers who graduated from the School of Education at the end of 2007. I conducted the study in four phases to generate information about the experiences of beginning secondary teachers at different stages of their initial teaching. I wanted to explore their sense of preparedness at the end of their initial teacher education, their experiences during the first month of teaching, after nine months of teaching during their first year and after nine months of teaching during their second year.

I used a structured questionnaire in the first phase to explore the teachers' perceptions of their initial teacher education programmes, and their sense of preparedness at the end of their initial teacher education. The questionnaire explored aspects of teaching for which the final-year preservice secondary teachers felt that their teacher education courses had adequately prepared them, and those they felt were inadequately covered during their initial teacher education.

Only 42 of the 121 final-year preservice secondary teachers could complete the questionnaire because the majority were on teaching practice in the provinces. From the 42 who completed the questionnaire, I invited 11 beginning teachers—four males and seven females—to participate in semistructured interviews in phases two, three and four of my study. In making this selection, I considered the courses they took at the School of Education, their provincial representation, gender and availability to participate in three interviews over a two-year period.

The first interview focused on the beginning secondary teachers' initial experiences as beginning teachers, their sense of preparedness for teaching and their confidence in applying various teaching skills and strategies during the first month of their teaching careers.

The second interview focused on their experiences during the first year of teaching, including their induction experiences and the kind of support they received from their respective secondary schools. The third interview focused on their experiences during the second year of teaching, especially how they had developed professionally as a teacher since the first year. It also examined their perceptions about the level of support they received from the schools over their first two years of teaching.

The data analysis process was based on the interpretive qualitative research methodology I adopted in the study. I used content analysis techniques to identify emerging themes, and then interpretive phenomenological analysis techniques to interpret and make meaning of the relationships within and between the key themes that emerged.

Findings

The findings of my study are summarised here under four broad categories, linked to the focus of my study and covering the beginning secondary teachers':
- sense of preparedness at the end of their initial teacher education (ITE)
- perceptions about their ITE programmes
- induction experiences
- professional learning experiences during the first two years of their teaching careers.

Sense of preparedness

It was evident from the 11 beginning secondary teachers' responses that they felt prepared to take on their teaching roles at the end of their ITE. However, they felt somewhat less confident about the planning and preparation of assessment tasks, preparing students' reports, keeping up with teaching plans, time management, meeting students' various learning needs, communicating with students and teachers, preparing teaching resources, standing in front of a class and teaching, classroom management and dealing with students' behaviour problems. The comments made by Zinnia[1] illustrate how the beginning secondary teachers felt during their first month of teaching:

> I am not really confident yet as a beginning teacher. I felt confident a bit, but I still feel nervous at times in my class. There are topics that I am not very confident to teach, and I am not yet really sure about how to go about assessing my students. I need help and advice from my HOD [head of department]. I sometimes approach my principal to help me overcome some of these challenges, when my colleagues could not help me.

Perceptions about their ITE

The 11 beginning secondary teachers identified three areas as the key strengths of their ITE programme: subject content, instructional planning and preparation skills, and teaching strategies and skills. They felt that the coverage of subject content in their ITE courses was adequate and provided them with a good basis for their subject content knowledge to begin teaching. However, they realised during their first year of teaching that they still needed to learn more about some topics in their subjects. They suggested that this could be due to content being covered superficially during their ITE, or not covered at all in some subject areas. They also reported that in some subjects there was a mismatch between the subject content they learnt through their ITE and the subject content in the secondary school curriculum. They suggested there was a need to update the content of some of their subjects to meet current standards. They felt less confident to teach some topics in their subjects for these reasons. This is illustrated in the comments made by Marcia:

---

1. To protect the identities of the participants pseudonyms are used in all cases.

> I think the teacher training programme at SICHE has prepared us well for teaching in our subject content, except that in some of our courses lecturers did not cover the content well. For example, in one of our units, our lecturer just rushed through the content, so we did not fully understand what we needed to learn in order to be able to teach it confidently to our students. I also found that some of the content was out of date.

The 11 beginning secondary teachers also believed that their ITE programme had prepared them well in terms of instructional planning and lesson preparations skills. The main challenges they initially faced in relation to the planning and preparation of their lessons were time constraints and lack of teaching resources: they all reported a general lack of these in their secondary schools. They also stated that they were assigned to teach two classes or more, and had at least one extra responsibility during their first two years of teaching. Some of them reported that they could not plan and prepare well for their lessons because of their heavy teaching loads:

> I think one of the main challenges for me is the lack of teaching resources, and textbooks. I do not know where to get them, or how to get them. For me as a beginning teacher and a probationer, I need the relevant teaching resources for my subjects and support from those responsible, so that I can perform well in my teaching, and pass my probation at the end of this year. I also find it difficult to prepare well for my lessons sometimes because of my heavy teaching load. I am only trained to teach maths and business studies, but now I am also teaching Science. (Henry)

The beginning secondary teachers also felt that their ITE programme prepared them well in terms of teaching strategies. They did lesson presentations through peer presentations and during their teaching practicum, which helped them develop confidence in relevant teaching skills. However, some of them indicated that they were not able to apply in practice some of the teaching strategies they learnt at the School of Education because they just learnt about them in theory:

> Our lecturers did not demonstrate to us how to teach certain aspects of our subjects ... the lecturers should demonstrate each teaching strategy first. They should also allow us time to practise, and give us enough feedback to help us improve before they ask us to do presentations during our peer teaching sessions. In education courses, although they covered the different methods of teaching well, they did not show us how to apply those teaching strategies in our specific subject areas. So, when I began my teaching now, I found it difficult to make the connection between the teaching strategies I learnt at the College, and how I should apply it in teaching my subject area. (Debbie)

Those who undertook the science and agriculture courses expressed the need for their lecturers to demonstrate more practical skills in their courses. They reported that they were not able to conduct some experiments and demonstrate certain practical skills confidently in their teaching because they were not given the opportunity to learn and practise these skills during their ITE. In essence, the beginning secondary teachers wanted to see more exemplary teaching and demonstration of relevant teaching strategies and skills for their specific subjects by their lecturers. Similarly, they would like associate teachers in schools to demonstrate exemplary teaching during their teaching practicum, so that they can learn from them:

> I would like to observe some of the classes taught by my associate teacher during my TE [teacher experience], before I begin teaching the classes assigned to me. But, I did not observe my associate teacher's classes during my last TE because she left me to take full responsibility of her class for the six weeks I was there, and only came to observe me three times and filled in the College TE Form. (Sophia)

They also had some concerns in relation to the duration of their teaching practice programme. For example, they felt that the teaching practicum period at the School of Education should be extended to a full semester in the final year. They were also concerned about the quality of feedback received from some associate teachers and lecturers. They reported that their associate teachers often just ticked the boxes in the School of Education Teaching Practice Observation Form without writing any comments. They also indicated that some of their supervisors from the college did the same:

> The feedback I received during my TE did not help me much. It was very brief. My associate teacher just ticked all the boxes in the College TE Observation Form, but did not write any comments. This does not tell me anything about my strengths and weaknesses and how I should improve. Even some lecturers do the same. (Zinnia)

They reiterated that such feedback was inadequate and did not tell them anything about their strengths and weaknesses and how they should improve. They would prefer more critical feedback that clearly pointed out their strengths and weaknesses and provided them with practical suggestions for improvement.

Induction experiences

The 11 beginning secondary teachers reported that their induction into their teaching roles was mainly informal—not through planned or official programmes. Instead, they were just introduced during their first staff meeting and allocated classes to teach. Then they were left alone to work with their heads of department (HODs) throughout their first two years of teaching. They learnt about their school's expectations and procedures through staff meetings and notices and from their experienced colleagues. There were no special meetings arranged for them during the first two years of their teaching careers:

> When I arrived here there was no one assigned to meet me. There was no induction programme organised for us new teachers at this school. So, I just approached my HOD because I believe he is the one

responsible for my subject at this school, and we decided on which class that I should teach, then I went on and prepared for my lessons and began attending my classes. There was no special meeting for us new teachers or anything like that. (Eugenie)

Although the beginning secondary teachers reported that they were not formally assigned a mentor to work with during their first nine months of teaching, some of them said they viewed their HODs as mentors. They sought help and support from their HODs because there were no formal systems in place at their schools to provide them with the kind of support they needed. The comments made by Sophia show that she viewed her HOD as her mentor:

> There was no formal induction or mentoring support since we last talked. I just went ahead with my teaching and just consulted my HOD whenever I needed help. My HOD was like my mentor since I started to teach at the beginning of this year.

In spite of the lack of formal induction and mentoring at their schools, they all spoke highly of the level of informal support they received from their experienced colleagues. They all felt that the staff at their schools were very supportive and willingly offered them advice. Their main source of support during their first two years was from their experienced colleagues and HODs. They also reported that although they did not receive enough formal feedback about their teaching from their HODs or principals, they did get informal feedback from their colleagues, students and some parents. The positive comments they received through informal feedback enhanced their confidence and motivated them to do even better in their teaching roles:

> I received informal feedback from my colleagues who think that I am a good teacher. My students also tell me that my lessons are interesting. I feel good about such feedback and that motivates me to do better each time I teach. (Doris)

It was evident from the beginning secondary teachers' responses that they needed someone to "go to" and "talk to" whenever they needed help during the first two years of their teaching careers. Almost all of them indicated that one-to-one mentoring was their preferred mode of support. They also indicated that they would prefer to work alongside a mentor or an experienced teacher in their own subject areas for at least the first year of their teaching careers:

> I would like a senior teacher in my subject to work closely with me and assist me before I work on my own. I would like my senior teacher to observe my teaching and give me regular feedback too, so that I can prepare well for when the Ministry of Education staff will come and observe me for my full registration. (Marcia)

The 11 beginning secondary teachers reported that they were not fully informed about the registration process for probationers during the first two years of their teaching careers. They were not yet fully registered as secondary teachers towards the end of their second year of teaching. The majority had had at least one observation done by officers from their education authority at that time:

> I am not registered yet, although they observed my lesson once so far for this purpose. I am still waiting for my confirmation letter from the MEHRD. I am still waiting on my principal to follow up the matter with the MEHRD. In fact, I am not aware of the requirements for full registration of new teachers. So, I am just waiting for my letter at the moment. When I receive the letter then I know that I am confirmed. I think such practice is not good enough. We should be fully informed about the registration process right at the beginning, or when we are still at the College. At the moment most of us probationers do not have any idea about what the teacher registration process really involves, the time frame, number of lesson observations, etc. (Henry)

The beginning secondary teachers reiterated that they needed support and advice during the first two years of their teaching careers on various aspects of their teaching roles, including subject content, teaching approaches, teaching resources, school procedures and expectations and the requirements for full registration. Overall, they needed support in all aspects of their teaching, both inside and outside the classroom.

Professional learning experiences

The beginning secondary teachers noticed a difference in their level of confidence in and understanding of their teaching roles as they progressed from the first to the second year of teaching. They felt they had developed a better understanding of their curriculum areas, how students learn, how to assess students' learning and how to develop better working relationships with other colleagues. They believed that informal support systems in schools had helped their learning, despite the absence of formal induction and professional support.

It was evident from these responses that their professional learning was supported through collaboration with experienced colleagues and HODs, and that informal dialogue with colleagues was the main source of support for their professional learning during their first two years:

> I learnt a lot from my HOD and other colleagues, whom I sought advice from whenever I needed help with my teaching. They help me by sharing their experiences and giving me advice. I always see my HOD about my teaching programme before I teach. My HOD also provides advice about how I should go about teaching a certain topic. This helped me a lot in my teaching and gives me more confidence in my teaching. (Marcia)

There was evidence to suggest that the beginning secondary teachers gained more confidence in their teaching roles as they became more familiar with the processes and procedures at their schools. They also became more satisfied with their teaching roles as they developed a collegial relationship with other staff, especially at the department level. They also reported that their professional learning was enhanced through self-reflection on their previous learning and teaching experiences. They believed that they improved their teaching by reflecting on what they learnt during their ITE and their teaching practices. Their teaching experiences in the first year also contributed to their professional learning during their second year of teaching, as they reflected upon their previous experience and improved on their weaknesses:

> I think I have improved a lot in my understanding of my subject content and teaching because I reflect on my previous experience in teaching the same topics last year and try to improve where necessary. I teach the way I do now based on my own experience of what my students enjoy and how they learned last year. (Jeremy)

Although the five community high schools where they were posted had no scheduled professional development programmes for beginning teachers, the beginning secondary teachers were encouraged to attend workshops organised by the Curriculum Development Centre, their education authorities and other nongovernment organisations:

> I attended workshops on assessment, counselling, and environment. These workshops were very useful and relevant to my teaching and professional development. I was able to improve in my assessment practices, how to deal with student problems, and how to help students to take care of their school environment. As you can see, we did some cleaning and landscaping of the school surroundings. (Doris)

They also reported participating in school activities that involved them in working closely with experienced teachers, their HODs, principals and deputy principals during their second year of teaching. For instance, being a class teacher required them to meet with their principals and other class teachers to discuss matters relating to students' learning and behaviour. This improved their understanding, as illustrated in the comments made by Paul:

> Being a class teacher I am required to meet with other teachers to discuss matters relating to the progress and behaviour of our students. So far, we have had two professional conversations. This helped me to understand my students better, in how they learn and behave.

The beginning secondary teachers felt strongly that their schools should have formal induction and professional development programmes in place for beginning teachers. They needed proper guidance and support as soon as they arrived at their schools, so that they could settle down and get on with their teaching roles quickly and further develop the knowledge and skills they learnt through their ITE. They felt that the MEHRD, education authorities and school principals should work together to put in place formal induction programmes for beginning teachers. They were also of the opinion that the School of Education should continue to play a role in beginning teachers' professional learning and development during their first two years of teaching.

The beginning secondary teachers had not taken the initiative to share their thoughts with their HODs or principals. They reported that they just shared their concerns among themselves because they felt they were just "junior" teachers and should not question the decision and actions taken by their "seniors", or those in authority. Such views may be attached to cultural beliefs and values that are inherent in Solomon Islands culture, whereby children are not allowed to question their parents, and young people their elders or those in authority.

Discussion

The findings of this study reflect the perceptions and experiences of the 11 beginning secondary teachers who participated in the study. They highlight a number of key issues that have important implications for teacher educators, education policy makers, education authorities, school leaders and teachers in the Solomon Islands. The summary of findings in the following section is based on my preliminary data analysis. I was still in the process of finalising the findings of my study and their implications for teacher education, induction and professional development practices in the Solomon Islands when this chapter was due for publication. As a result, the summary below is tentative and needs to be developed in greater depth.

Key findings

Initial teacher education experiences

The beginning secondary teachers were generally satisfied that their ITE programmes at the School of Education provided them with the foundational knowledge and skills they needed to begin their teaching careers. However, they reported that they felt less prepared in some aspects of their teaching roles and needed guidance and support from the school community. This supports the notion that teacher learning does not stop at the end of their ITE (Loughran, 2007). Rather, it is a lifelong process (Murdoch, 1979). It was evident from the findings of this study that the 11 beginning secondary teachers needed guidance and support to enhance their sense of preparedness and confidence to teach throughout the first two years of their teaching careers.

They all emphasised the need for teacher educators and associate teachers to model best practice in their ITE courses and during their teaching practicum. Their responses indicated that they valued an iterative process of learning, involving observation and reflection, trial of teaching strategies and skills, through which they are given adequate feedback. This, they believed, could help them develop more confidence when applying specific teaching skills in their teaching. The lack of adequate opportunity for them to be involved in such a process during their ITE and teaching practicum had a negative impact on their perceptions about their ITE and teaching practicum experiences.

Induction and professional learning experiences

It was evident from the findings of this study that the beginning secondary teachers' unfamiliarity with school expectations, policies and procedures caused them to feel anxious and less confident at the beginning of their teaching careers. However, their level of confidence and satisfaction in their teaching roles improved as they became more familiar with their schools' expectations and procedures, and developed collegial working relationships with their experienced colleagues. This is in line with the findings of previous studies on beginning teachers' experiences conducted in other countries, including New Zealand (Anthony, Bell, Haigh, & Kane, 2007), Australia (Loughran, Brown, & Doecke, 2001) and Portugal (Flores, 2006).

Their induction into their teaching roles was mainly informal because there were no planned or official induction programmes. They learnt about school expectations and procedures through informal dialogue with their experienced colleagues, and this contributed to their professional learning and motivation to teach. Their professional learning and development depended on collaboration with experienced colleagues and self-reflection on their previous experiences. These experiences were somewhat different from those of beginning teachers in New Zealand, who go through a formal induction programme, with support from mentors/tutor teachers for the first two years of their teaching careers (Anthony et al., 2007; Langdon, 2007).

The beginning secondary teachers believed that schools should have formal induction and professional development opportunities for beginning teachers. They suggested that the MEHRD, education authorities and school principals should work together to ensure that formal induction and professional development programmes for teachers are available in schools. They also suggested that the School of Education should continue to play a role in pre-service teachers' professional learning and development during their first year of teaching.

They indicated that one-to-one mentoring was the best mode of professional support for beginning teachers. They believed that if they worked alongside a mentor—preferably an experienced teacher in their own subject areas—for at least the first year of their teaching careers, it would enhance their professional learning and development. This view supports Vygotsky's (1978) sociocultural theory of learning, which emphasises the need for apprentice learners to receive guidance and support from mentors, or more knowledgeable others, in order for them to successively achieve more complex skills, understanding and, ultimately, independent competence in specific areas of learning. The findings of previous research confirm that it is essential for beginning teachers to be exposed to good role models, as it helps them to build their sense of confidence and promote their learning during the initial years of their teaching careers (Langdon, 2007).

Lack of teaching resources—or specialised classrooms for subjects like science, industrial arts, home economics and agriculture—had a negative impact on the beginning secondary teachers' ability to apply some of the knowledge and teaching strategies they learnt during their ITE. The findings of this study showed that these teachers assumed the same responsibilities as their experienced colleagues, right from the beginning of their first year of teaching. These responsibilities meant it was more difficult to spend time learning how to teach well. The beginning teachers' heavy teaching loads negatively affected their ability to learn in and from their teaching practice. This is similar to the findings of other studies, which found that beginning teachers' professional learning and development are not always supported by their school culture (Feiman-Nemser, 2001; Kagan, 1992; Wideen, Mayer-Smith, & Moon, 1998).

The 11 beginning secondary teachers also had very little knowledge about the registration process for probationers during the first two years of their teaching careers. They were not yet fully registered up to the end of the second year of their teaching careers.

Implications for educational researchers, policy makers, teacher educators and school leaders

This study found a lack of formal induction and professional support for beginning secondary teachers in secondary schools. Research evidence suggests that the quality of teaching and learning and the level of student achievement in schools are directly linked to the quality of teachers (Darling-Hammond & Bransford, 2005; Flores, 2004). If beginning teachers are to further develop the knowledge and skills they learnt during their initial teacher education, and deliver quality instruction for students, then they should be provided with effective learning opportunities and support during their early years of teaching. The quality of professional support provided for beginning teachers can promote teacher effectiveness as well as influence how long teachers will remain in the teaching profession (Anthony et al., 2007). Therefore, education policy makers in the Solomon Islands need to ensure that the necessary resources are invested in programmes that provide induction and professional support and development opportunities for teachers in secondary schools.

Ideally, the Solomon Islands needs to establish a learning continuum to advance teachers' professional learning and development, from ITE, to induction and throughout teachers' careers. This is vitally important so that teachers can be continually supported to enhance their teaching knowledge and skills. Such a continuum should adopt sound pedagogical practices that promote teacher learning and professional development through an iterative learning process, relevant to the Solomon Islands' context. ITE, induction and professional development programmes should allow teachers to reflect on their practices and learn from their previous experiences, with support from knowledgeable others.

Such programmes need to be well resourced, co-ordinated and effectively managed in order to be successful. This requires further investigation, proper planning and the collaborative effort of all stakeholders in the Solomon Islands school system. It is also important to ensure that whatever system the Solomon Islands chooses to adopt to support the professional learning and development of teachers, it does not add an extra burden to the current workload of teachers and school principals. This will certainly be a challenge for education policy makers, teacher educators and school leaders in the Solomon Islands. However, it is a worthy goal to work towards, if the Solomon Islands aspires to improve the quality of teaching and learning in its school system.

The call for mentoring and modelling by the beginning secondary teachers in this study indicates a need for professional support for beginning teachers. This does not mean having "perfect" role models, or mentors who make no mistakes—such role models and mentors would be hard to find anywhere. Support is essential for beginning teachers' professional learning and development, and can enhance their confidence in their teaching roles. The fact that beginning teachers' learning takes place in real-life school settings means that the kind of teacher models they are exposed to can influence their perceptions about their teaching roles and practices. Principals and teachers in schools where beginning teachers are posted are in the most appropriate position to support beginning teachers' learning and professional development. Therefore, it would be logical to invest the necessary resources in schools so that principals and experienced teachers can offer appropriate support for the beginning teachers they recruit each year.

The lack of teaching resources and poor work conditions highlighted in this study could also have a drastic effect on the professional learning and development of beginning teachers in schools. Research on teacher retention has shown that poor work conditions, including lack of teaching resources, do not only affect teachers' teaching performance or students' learning achievements, but they are major factors leading to teachers leaving the profession (Anthony et al., 2007; Flores, 2006). Teacher retention may not seem to be an issue in the Solomon Islands at the moment, compared to countries like Australia and New Zealand (Kane & Fontaine, 2007; Loughran et al., 2001). Nevertheless, it could become an issue in the future if the challenges faced by teachers in relation to poor work conditions and lack of teaching resources are left unaddressed for too long. The beginning secondary teachers in this study were satisfied with their teaching roles, despite the many challenges they faced in relation to poor work conditions, heavy workload and lack of teaching resources. However, the effect of work conditions on teacher performance and satisfaction in the Solomon Islands needs to be explored in depth to ascertain teachers' levels of satisfaction at different stages of their teaching careers. The adequacy of teaching resources in Solomon Islands schools also needs further investigation, so that the perceived lack of resources can be adequately addressed.

The many challenges experienced by the Solomon Islands beginning secondary teachers who participated in this study, including the delay in their full registration, might reflect the leadership of the Solomon Islands school system. Although teachers are at the front line of teaching in the classroom, school principals—in collaboration with school board chairpersons—and education authorities are responsible for setting clear visions and expectations for their schools. School principals and school boards are responsible for the professional culture within a school and the means by which a school can achieve specific standards and expectations (De Vita, 2007). Thus, the lack of effective and sustained induction and teacher professional development programmes in schools may be a reflection of the type of school culture and quality of leadership that are prevalent in a school system. Given public expectations for beginning teachers to perform like their experienced colleagues, right from day one of their teaching careers, it is vitally important that education leaders create the kind of environment that enables teachers to perform their best in schools (Darling-Hammond, 2006). Stanulis and Floden (2009) have pointed out that novices with inadequate support need about three to seven years of teaching before they can reach their full potential as teachers.

An implication is that Solomon Islands schools need leaders who can ensure an enriching school culture for beginning teachers so that they can receive the kind of support they need. Principals have the responsibility to ensure the provision of induction and professional development programmes for teachers in schools. They should also be responsible for the assessment of beginning teachers' performance prior to their full registration, and ensure they are registered before the end of their probationary period. The relationship between the kind of school culture available for beginning teachers in the Solomon Islands school system and the school leadership requires further investigation. There is also a need to explore the process involved in the full registration of probationary teachers and the quality of judgement made about probationers' teaching performance before they are fully registered.

The relationship between beginning teacher induction and leadership also warrants further investigation. Principals have a responsibility to provide an induction programme and the final assessment of the beginning teacher prior to full registration. Examination of how judgements are made about beginning teachers would provide insight into the quality of early-career fully registered teachers. They also provide the learning context. The quality of beginning teacher induction determines the quality of school experiences, and so it is important to know more about the effect of this relationship and about the schools that are inducting beginning teachers, along with their practices and needs. Should all schools induct beginning teachers? To make a commitment to quality, there is a need to examine how policy and individual schools can ensure all beginning teachers experience sound induction and learning as they develop their pedagogy and identity as professionals.

Conclusion

The findings of this study point to the fact that beginning teachers want and need professional support and guidance during their early years of teaching in order to become successful in their teaching roles. The lack of formal support and guidance, coupled with lack of teaching resources experienced by the beginning secondary teachers who participated in this study, mean that they are unlikely to become effective in their teaching at the beginning of their careers—or throughout their teaching for that matter. The challenge for education policy makers, education researchers, teacher educators, school principals and teachers is to ensure that beginning teachers are provided with appropriate learning opportunities and professional support during their ITE and at the beginning of their teaching careers.

Current research points to the need for such learning opportunities for teachers to be grounded on sound pedagogical and ethical teaching practices that are relevant to teachers' sociocultural context, supported by a collaborative school learning environment. Undoubtedly this is a challenging task for education policy makers and leaders. However, if these issues and challenges are not addressed, they will continue to have a negative impact on the quality of teaching and learning in Solomon Islands schools. Effective school leadership, coupled with a school culture that promotes effective teacher learning, can have a positive impact on beginning teachers' learning and professional development. The findings of this study have important implications for the improvement of teacher education and professional development practices, and for school leadership and school culture in Solomon Islands secondary schools.

References

Anthony, G., Bell, B., Haigh, M., & Kane, R. (2007, April). *Induction into the profession: Findings from New Zealand beginning teachers*. Paper presented to the American Educational Research Association, Chicago.

Darling-Hammond, L. (2006). Constructing 21st century teacher education. *Journal of Teacher Education, 57*, 300–314.

Darling-Hammond, L., & Bransford, J. (2005). *Preparing teachers for a changing world: What teachers should learn and be able to do*. San Francisco: Jossey-Bass.

De Vita, C. (2007, October). *Leadership: The bridge to better learning*. Paper presented at the Wallace Foundation's national conference, New York.

Feiman-Nemser, S. (2001). From preparation to practice: Designing a continuum to strengthen and sustain teaching. *Teachers College Record, 103*(6), 1013–1055.

Flores, M. A. (2004). The impact of school culture and leadership on new teachers' learning in the workplace. *International Journal of Leadership in Education, 7*(4), 297–318.

Flores, M. A. (2006). Being a novice teacher in two different settings: Struggles, continuities, and discontinuities. *Teachers College Record, 108*(10), 2021–2052.

Kagan, V. F. (1992). Implications of research on teacher beliefs. *Educational Psychologist, 27*(1), 65–90.

Kane, R. G., & Fontaine, S. (2007, April). *Choosing to become (and to remain) a secondary teacher in New Zealand: Findings from two national studies*. Paper presented at the annual meeting of the American Educational Research Association, Chicago.

Langdon, F. J. (2007). *Beginning teacher learning and professional development: An analysis of induction programmes*. Hamilton: University of Waikato.

Loughran, J. (2007). Enacting a pedagogy of teacher education. In T. Russell & J. Loughran (Eds.), *Enacting a pedagogy of teacher education: Values, relationships and practices* (pp. 1–15). New York: Routledge.

Loughran, J., Brown, J., & Doecke, B. (2001). Continuities and discontinuities: The transition from pre-service to first-year teaching. *Teachers & Teaching, 7*(1), 7–23.

Murdoch, R. T. (1979, June). *Teacher induction: The current situation.* Paper presented at the one-day seminar of school principals, Palmerston North.

SICHE. (1998). *School of education handbook.* Honiara: Author.

SICHE. (2009). *Teacher education handbook.* Honiara: Author.

Stanulis, R. N., & Floden, R. E. (2009). Intensive mentoring as a way to help beginning teachers develop balanced instruction. *Journal of Teacher Education, 60*(2), 112–122.

Taylor, L., & Pollard, B. (2004). *School of education review and development plan.* Honiara: Solomon Islands College of Higher Education.

Vygotsky, L. S. (1978). *Voices of the mind: A socio-cultural approach to mediated action.* Cambridge, MA: Harvard University Press.

Wideen, M., Mayer-Smith, J., & Moon, B. (1998). A critical analysis of the research on learning to teach: Making the case for an ecological perspective on inquiry. *Review of Education Research, 68*(2), 130–178.

Wrightson, T. (2005). *Solomon Islands NZAID education support for national teacher training and development programme: Inception report.* Auckland: ANZDEC.

Patricia Rodie

Patricia was born in Malukuna village in Central Guadalcanal. She attended Betivatu primary school and Su'u secondary school then moved to Goroka Teachers' College where she received a Diploma in Teaching (Secondary), majoring in English and home economics. She taught secondary home economics at Selwyn College before completing a BEd at the University of the South Pacific in Suva and a masters degree at Curtin University in Western Australia. She was then appointed to the position of lecturer in education and home economics at the School of Education, SICHE where she became Head of School in 2004. She left to take up a doctoral scholarship to the University of Waikato where she is currently completing her thesis. Patricia is married with three children and outside education enjoys gardening, listening to country/gospel music, craftwork and reading.

SECTION TWO

SCHOOL LEADERSHIP

CHAPTER 4
Effective School Leadership in the Solomon Islands

Donald Malasa
Ministry of Education and Human Resources Development, Solomon Islands

Introduction

The need to establish effective leadership and management of schools in the Solomon Islands' education system is a long-standing issue and has existed since the country gained political independence in 1978. The issue has been further exacerbated by the rapid establishment of the community high schools (CHS) throughout the country since 1995, with many of these schools staffed by inadequately trained teachers and inexperienced principals (MEHRD, 2004). Such rapid expansion of the secondary system, although made with good intentions (Sikua, 2002), has led to a deteriorating state of leadership and management in most of the schools throughout the country, and this issue is high among the concerns heard by the Ministry of Education and Human Resources Development (MEHRD) from parents and the general public.

There is no previous research on school leadership in the Solomon Islands. Although there is a wide range of international literature focusing on effective school leadership, some of the findings are not valid in the context of a developing nation such as the Solomon Islands. There is a clear need for research that addresses the issues of this specific context. This chapter reports on the findings of an intensive research project that explored the perceptions held by Solomon Islands principals about the factors that inhibit effective school leadership and management in their schools. It discusses the issues raised and argues that the establishment of professional development programmes for newly appointed and longer serving principals is a key priority. Such programmes would enhance principals' leadership capability and create a more conducive learning environment in schools.

The research process

My research began with a review of the relevant international literature and research on the issue, mostly on school leadership issues in the United States, the United Kingdom, Europe, Australia, New Zealand and other Pacific Islands. From this I identified my major research question: In the opinion of principals, what issues inhibit effective leadership at school level in the Solomon Islands?

The research data were gathered using qualitative methods that identify the assumptions and beliefs of those involved in the study. A sample of five participants was selected from five schools, representing CHS and senior provincial secondary schools in two provinces, and Honiara. I interviewed each of the five principals using a semistructured interview format and analysed the transcripts using a thematic analysis approach. This research fieldwork was carried out in the Solomon Islands in August 2006.

The findings: Issues affecting school leadership

My research uncovered a number of issues that principals believe inhibit effective school leadership. These issues fell into three major categories:
- systemic issues
- sociocultural and school–community relationships
- geographical and political issues.

The systemic issues included a lack of initial training and support for ongoing professional learning, unfavourable conditions of service, the poor quality of teachers' professional practice, poor school facilities and infrastructure, poor administrative infrastructure, lack of appropriate and adequate financial resources, lack of support personnel, policy and systemic issues, social and cultural issues and issues pertaining to school–community partnerships.

The sociocultural and community issues included the ways in which traditional cultural and social practices can inhibit school leaders. The geographic, sociocultural and political issues are outside the control of educational leaders but have a significant impact on the work of schools. All of these issues need to be seriously considered by policy makers and educational leaders and administrators at the national, provincial, community and school levels, because they have the potential to impede effective educational leadership in the Solomon Islands if not adequately addressed.

Systemic issues

Lack of preprincipalship preparation

Lack of initial preparation and support for ongoing professional learning for school principals poses an enormous challenge to the growth and development of the leadership capacity of the principals, teachers and students, as well as the whole school system in the

Solomon Islands. It has been identified as one of the inhibiting factors not only by school principals in this study but also by parents and members of school communities (MEHRD, 2004, 2005a, 2005b.). Lack of initial preparation for principals could limit their ability in critical engagement and their understanding of how to effectively lead and manage their schools; this was reflected in the superficial nature of the participants' responses, which lacked in-depth analysis of the research questions. Most of the school principals were promoted straight from their classrooms and without initial leadership and management training. Most school principals would have completed initial teacher training at the Solomon Islands College of Higher Education (SICHE), the University of the South Pacific or other regional universities and institutions with diplomas and first degrees. Very few have masters or other postgraduate qualifications in educational leadership, management and administration.

These issues highlight the need for school principals in the Solomon Islands to receive both initial leadership preparation and ongoing support to equip them academically and professionally for their leadership positions at their schools. This is even more important if they have never been a deputy before and have very limited experience of leading and managing a school. Without such initial training to equip them for their demanding leadership roles, most of these newly appointed school principals (and even experienced ones) could be overwhelmed by the demands of their new roles—from students, parents, communities and the national government—and, according to Paterson and West-Burnham (2005), could begin to feel pressured and isolated. This was evident with most principals in the study. Interestingly, the literature makes numerous references to the need for ongoing professional learning but is largely silent on the matter of developing resilience, even though this appears to be an emerging feature of current studies of highly effective principals.

Although most of the principals in the study had the skills needed for the routine operation and management of their schools, there is a great need for principals to be effective problem solvers as well. A lot of the issues alluded to during the interviews could have been avoided or resolved had the principals been more creative in addressing them. Problem-solving skills, according to Goertz (2000), require creativity and investigative skills, which are an integral component of effective leadership.

Unless they are given initial and ongoing professional learning opportunities in leadership, most newly appointed and serving principals will find it very difficult to cope with the demands of their role. Such initial training will not only provide the opportunity for newly appointed principals to dedicate time for analysis and reflection, but can also allow them to establish open dialogue with fellow principals. This, according to Goertz (2000), is the basis for meaning making and problem solving—an approach that clearly helps reduce the principals' sense of isolation. Such reduction in isolation is also likely to contribute to an increase in resilience.

In addition to initial leadership preparation, the ongoing support of staff and colleagues, the school board and the Provincial Education Board is essential for effective leadership of schools. This includes the continued support and encouragement of immediate family and members of the school community. Such ongoing support from staff and colleagues, school boards and the provincial education authorities should provide an avenue for school principals to develop and share their visions of the school (Harris et al., 2003; Leithwood, Janti, & Steinbach, 1999).

Unfavourable conditions of service

My research found that the salary levels of teachers in the Solomon Islands are very low compared to those for other professions in the country. As a result, school principals are often faced with ongoing industrial action by teachers' unions over the conditions of service of their teachers. These issues are clearly of great importance to the teachers, and they divert the attention of most school principals from their core leadership roles, even though they are not responsible for salary setting. This can lead to low morale and general lack of motivation of teachers, especially in boarding schools (MEHRD, 2004), and can be an obstacle to effective leadership and improvement in the schools (Everard, 1986).

The study revealed that the current teachers' salary and reward system in the Solomon Islands is unrealistic and was regarded by the principals in the study as an obstacle to effective leadership and improvement in their schools. It does not reward principals and teachers according to their contribution, and all five principals in the study expressed their frustration at their inability to give tangible recognition to staff and teachers' outstanding performance. This is because schools and education authorities, unlike their counterparts in business and industry, do not have the freedom to decide on the appropriate salary and remuneration package for their principals and teachers. This is the function of the Teaching Service Commission of the MEHRD.

The unfavourable conditions of service and accommodation and working conditions of staff can be an obstacle to attracting more qualified and experienced teachers, especially to the schools in the rural parts of the country, and can have an influence on the effective leadership of these schools. This is because staff and teachers are also important resources for effective leadership and management in organisations such as schools (Barker, 2001; Day, 2000; Harris & Chapman, 2002; Kotter, 1998), and one of the key characteristics of effective leaders is that they are valued by those in authority (Love, 2005; SEDL, 2005).

My findings also show that the recruitment of quality teachers can contribute to the effective distribution of leadership and helps to avoid creating gaps between the middle and senior leadership teams of the schools, which can lead to the principals spending disproportionately large amounts of time on curriculum and instructional issues and very little time on leadership issues. Low rates of salary make it difficult to attract quality teachers at this level.

Poor facilities and infrastructure

My findings show that the state of the facilities and infrastructure of a school can significantly affect the morale of those who work in it (including both the principal and the teachers) and can contribute to leadership issues and challenges. As supported by various reports on the Solomon Islands education system (MEHRD, 2004, 2005a, 2005b; Sikua, 2002), the lack of proper buildings and facilities is one of the biggest issues most schools face, and is one of the factors contributing to the difficulties in attracting well qualified staff, including principals. Such poor facilities in the schools can also result in lack of effective delivery of teaching and learning to the students, and can affect the general leadership and management of the schools.

Lack of communication

Schools depend on communication with the MEHRD for updates on policy issues and for professional advice. However, all five school principals in the study complained about the lack of basic communication and office equipment, such as computer, photocopier, fax machine and telephone. All except one lacked telephone and Internet connections, and were missing out on vital communication and information from the MEHRD and other organisations. This was clearly a major issue, especially for the schools located far from the MEHRD's offices. They lacked vital information and notices from the MEHRD regarding changes in education policy, job opportunities, inservice training and scholarships opportunities

(MEHRD, 2004, 2005a, 2005b; Sikua, 2002). Most schools in the study had to rely on their respective provincial education offices to convey such vital information from the MEHRD and other organisations. However, this in turn depended on the capacity of these authorities to handle such vital information and relay it to the schools. All participants were able to give numerous examples of the failure of this communication chain.

Lack of office equipment

Another concern expressed by the principals in the study was the effect a lack of basic office equipment—such as computers, photocopying and duplicating machines—in their schools had on their leadership activities. Although it can be argued that schools can survive without computers, the fact that some curriculum resources are stored on CDs has in practice made computers essential for all schools. Principals claimed that the absence of this basic equipment had affected the effective delivery of some of the components of the school curriculum, which rely on photocopying and printing the teaching and learning resources. This can be a challenge to these principals' leadership abilities and effectiveness.

Lack of financial resources

All the principals in the study spoke of the importance of the annual grants their schools receive from the MEHRD and (in some schools) their provincial governments. Having support staff to assist in the running of their schools was also important. Although this can be regarded as an administrative and management matter, the availability of financial resources can have a significant impact on leadership activities. Again, this issue indicates a general lack of capacity and effectiveness at the macro and middle levels of educational management in the Ministry and the provincial offices. The inevitable consequence of this is principals spending alarming amounts of time attempting to access funding to which they were entitled in the first place. From a community perspective, the effectiveness of the principals is often judged by the amount of money they are able to raise. As all principals need to meet certain community expectations regarding appropriate performance levels, this places principals in a dilemma that further reduces their capacity to focus on leadership and learning in their schools.

Lack of logistics and support personnel

Most principals interviewed expressed the need to employ support staff at the school so that they can devote more time to their leadership roles. Four out of the five principals stated that due to lack of support staff at the school, most of their time was spent doing administrative work and the routine day-to-day running of the school. Thus, at the end of the day there was no time left for the principals to engage in meaningful leadership and management tasks of a more strategic nature, develop long-term goals for the school and spend more time with staff and colleagues. The need to employ nonteaching staff to assist with administrative tasks at the school is more evident in the boarding secondary schools. Nonteaching administrative staff are able to take care of administrative and financial management matters, and the daily routine of boarding and logistical matters, thus freeing the principals to concentrate more on leadership issues affecting the schools.

Systemic policy issues

The current organisation and management of the Solomon Islands education system can result in issues of accountability and responsibility that have a substantial impact on the leadership of schools (Bray, 1991; MEHRD, 2004, 2005a; Sikua, 2002). In particular, if there is a clash between national and provincial policies, this can distract the principals' attention from their main duties of leading and managing their schools and can prevent them from effectively leading their schools. It also creates a dilemma for the principals over which policy they should follow, and can distract them from time when they should be concentrating on their leadership role. The confusion has also created further distractions resulting from professional and legal ambiguities. This issue, according to Bray (1991), is partly the result of the current decentralised education system. The ambiguity and lack of clear accountability in this system also have the potential to result in issues relating to the distribution of financial resources and the recruitment of teachers and personnel, and can lead to the school system operating inefficiently.

Sociocultural and community issues

The influence of the Melanesian "wantok" system and the associated social and cultural obligations on leadership can potentially inhibit school principals from effectively leading their schools. The wantok system places an absolute obligation on individuals to support their extended family before others. This can conflict with their professional obligation to treat everyone fairly and equitably. For example, one principal recounted how a relative had expected him to enrol his child in the school although he had not met the required standard for entry. Refusing this request violated cultural expectations. This is a substantial challenge, not only for the principals but for all leaders in the Solomon Islands. The findings of the study show that the influence of the traditional Solomon Islands cultures and social practices can inhibit effective school leadership and can contribute to the low participation of women in school leadership positions.

The findings revealed an influence of the traditional societal beliefs on the decisions of both the national and provincial education officers. I am talking here about what Southworth (1995) refers to as "the social conditioning which has tended to sustain male seniority, if not dominance in some schools" (p. 148). As explained above, the Solomon Islands is a country known to have strong cultural beliefs about gender roles, and therefore any study on the leadership performance of principals cannot ignore the societal and cultural context in which the organisation or institution is situated, because these factors can influence the thought and behaviour patterns of its leaders. A woman principal noted that it took her 10 years to achieve a principal's post while her male colleagues had taken two to five years. She attributed this to deeply embedded cultural beliefs that women were not leaders. Basically, leadership studies cannot be conducted without considering the societal values of the culture in which the leadership is situated (Chemers, 1997; Dimmock & Walker, 2002, 2005; Sergiovanni, 1991; Wong, 1998).

All the five principals interviewed spoke of the importance of maintaining school–community partnerships as a means of generating resources that are essential for effective schooling. In particular, they view the involvement of parents as crucial to their students' learning and their school's success. However, they also spoke of the need to be alert to issues relating to the involvement of parents and members of the school community that can affect their leadership of the school. These include the tendency of some members of the community to use their involvement with the school for personal political and financial gains, which can have implications for the principal's activities in terms of ensuring that these negative influences do not have a significant impact on the school.

Another important aspect is the principal's need to create a balance between addressing the needs of the school and the demands of their own family, parents and school communities. If they do not strike a balance, these competing areas of responsibility will challenge them professionally and physically, and will be a strain on their leadership roles at the school (Boris-Schacter, 2006).

Conclusion

The findings from my study offer interesting insights into the problems and dilemmas faced by each of the participants during the interviews, and give an indication of the depth of passion and commitment they offer to their schools. However, my conclusion on the basis of the literature review is that there are obvious omissions and silences in the interviews. Much of the information they offered concerns administrative and managerial aspects of their work. While I acknowledge that the majority of a principal's time is likely to be taken up by this type of work (Southworth, 2005), it seems that the participants have not dwelt at any length on the more leadership-oriented aspects of their work.

The issues inhibiting effective school leadership in the Solomon Islands can be best understood within the prevailing political, economic and sociocultural contexts (Davies, 1994; Dimmock & Walker, 2002) that exist in the Solomon Islands. This study contributes to an understanding of the issues and the possible influences of recent global trends, which can assist in further reforms of the leadership of schools and address the dearth of literature on school leadership in the Solomon Islands.

From a leadership perspective, the findings of the study support (in a limited way) recent reports of studies conducted in 2004 (MEHRD, 2005a) that attributed the decline in the effectiveness of school-based leadership and management in the Solomon Islands schools to the lack of personal leadership qualities and administrative competencies, and to the leadership styles of school principals. The general lack of initial training and ongoing support for the professional learning of principals is a key leadership issue in the Solomon Islands that could limit the principals' capacity for critical engagement and understanding of how to lead their schools effectively. This concern at the lack of initial training for school principals was also highlighted by Puamau (1998) and Kelep-Malpo (2003) in their studies of school principals in Fiji and Papua New Guinea, respectively.

The findings also highlight systemic issues, such as unfavourable conditions of service and lack of appropriate and adequate financial resourcing, which can lead to low morale. Furthermore, the lack of systemic clarity—and apparently competing elements of the organisation of the Solomon Islands education system as a result of the current decentralised education system—has resulted in problems related to financial resourcing and personnel management that appear to result in the inefficient operation of schools (Bray, 1991). This has further resulted in accountability and responsibility issues (Bray, 1991; MEHRD, 2004, 2005a; Sikua, 2002) and has distracted the principals' attention from their main duty of effectively leading their schools.

Another finding of the study is that the issue of geographical isolation is a great concern for schools in the isolated and rural parts of the country. The geographical location of schools and their isolation (Peca, 2003) create individual and contextually specific challenges for principals. The study also supported claims (Martin & Robertson, 2003; Mills, 1994; Sanders, 2006; Southworth, 2005) that the limited capacity of many parents and community members to have a significant impact on their children's education, and their limited capacity to contribute, results in further stresses for the principals and further detracts from their limited time for leadership.

The principals' narratives give clear evidence of the influence of the Melanesian wantok system, such that the associated social and cultural obligations can potentially inhibit most school principals from leading their schools effectively. Furthermore, the Solomon Islands is a country known to have strong cultural beliefs about gender roles, which can inhibit the participation of women in the leadership of schools. However, the study confirms the importance of principals maintaining school–community partnerships and a balance between addressing the needs of the school and the demands of their own family, parents and school communities (Boris-Schacter, 2006).

Despite the above findings, it seems to me that a major silence in the data I gathered from the principals concerns their focus on leadership—as opposed to management. It seems that a major issue is that principals in the Solomon Islands have not moved from a managerial to a leadership way of thinking. They appear to be firmly located in a managerial paradigm to the exclusion of leadership. As a result, they lack an in-depth, critical understanding of many of the issues affecting their leadership roles in their schools.

References

Barker, B. (2001). Do leaders matter? *Educational Review, 53*(1), 65–76. Retrieved 4 June 2005, from EBSCO host database.

Boris-Schacter, S. (2006). *Balanced leadership: How effective principals manage their work.* New York: Teachers College, Columbia University.

Bray, M. (Ed). (1991). *Ministries of education in small states: Case studies of organization and management.* London: Commonwealth Secretariat.

Chemers, M. M. (1997). *An integrated theory of leadership.* Mahwah, NJ: Lawrence Erlbaum.

Davies, L. (1994). *Beyond authoritarian school management: The challenge for transparency.* Derbyshire: Education Now Books.

Day, C. (2000). Effective leadership and reflective practice. *Reflective Practice, 1*(1), 113–127. Retrieved 3 May 2005, from EBSCO host database.

Dimmock, C., & Walker, A. (2002). Moving school leadership beyond its narrow boundaries: Developing a cross-cultural approach. In K. Leithwood & P. Hallinger (Eds.), *Second international handbook of educational leadership and administration* (pp. 167–202). Dordrecht, The Netherlands: Kluwer Academic.

Dimmock, C., & Walker, A. (2005). Developing leadership in context. In M. J. Coles & G. Southworth (Eds.), *Developing leadership: Creating the schools of tomorrow* (pp. 80–94). Buckinghamshire: Open University Press.

Everard, K. B. (1986). *Developing management in schools.* London: Basil Blackwell.

Goertz, J. (2000). Creativity: An essential component for effective leadership in today's schools. *Roeper Review, 22*(3), 158–163.

Harris, A., & Chapman, C. (2002). Democratic leadership for school in challenging contexts. *International Electronic Journal for Leadership in Learning, 6*(17). Retrieved 9 April 2005, from http://www.ucalgary.ca/~iejll

Harris, A., Day, C., Hopkins, D., Hadfield, M., Hargreaves, A., & Chapman, C. (2003). *Effective leadership for school improvements.* New York: Routledge Falmer.

Kelep-Malpo, K. D. (2003). *Gender and school leadership in the Papua New Guinea public school system.* Unpublished doctoral thesis, Victoria University of Wellington, Wellington.

Kotter, J. P. (1998). Winning at change. *Leader to Leader, 10*. Retrieved 2 October 2006, from http://www.leadertoleader.org

Leithwood, K., Janti, D., & Steinbach, R. (1999). *Changing leadership for changing times*. Buckinghamshire: Open University Press.

Love, C. T. (2005). Using both hands and heart for effective leadership. *Journal of Family and Consumer Sciences, 97*(2). Retrieved 6 June 2005, from http://proquest.umi.com.ezproxy.waikato.ac.nz

Martin, J., & Robertson, J. (2003). The induction of first-time principals in New Zealand programs design. *International Journal for Leadership in Learning, 7*(2). Retrieved 17 March 2005, from http://www.ucalgary.ca/~iejll

Mills, S. (1994). *Extending the learning community: Involving parents and families in schools*. SSTA Research Centre Report 94–09. Retrieved 23 March 2005, from http://www.ssta.sk.ca/research/parent_involvement/94-09.htm#wipf

MEHRD. (2004). *Education strategic plan 2004–2006*. Honiara: Author.

MEHRD. (2005a). *2004 annual report*. Honiara: Author.

MEHRD. (2005b). *Education corporate plan 2006–2008*. Honiara: Author.

Paterson, F., & West-Burnham, J. (2005). Developing beginning leadership. In M. J. Coles & G. Southworth (Eds.), *Developing leadership: Creating the schools of tomorrow* (pp. 108–126). Buckinghamshire: Open University Press.

Peca, K. (2003). Rural school administrators: Insider versus outsider approaches to challenges. *Catalyst for Change, 33*, 20–25. Retrieved 20 June 2006, from http://wilsontxt.hwwilson.com/pdfhtml/03961/LETJV/VSI.htm

Puamau, P. (1998). The principalship in Fiji secondary schools: A critical post-colonial perspective. In L. Ehrich & K. Knight (Eds.), *Leadership in crisis? Restructuring principled practice: Essays on contemporary educational leadership* (pp. 152–166). Brisbane: Port Press.

Sanders, M. G. (2006). *Building school–community partnerships: Collaboration for student success*. Thousand Oaks, CA: Corwin Press.

SEDL. (2005). *Leadership characteristics that facilitate school change*. Southwest Educational Development Laboratory. Retrieved 26 September 2006, from http://www.sedl.org/change/leadership/history.html

Sergiovanni, T. (1991). *The principalship: A reflective practice perspective* (2nd ed.). Needham Heights, MA: Allyn & Bacon.

Sikua, D. D. (2002). *The decentralisation of education in a developing country: A case of community high schools in the Solomon Islands*. Unpublished doctoral thesis, University of Waikato, Hamilton.

Southworth, G. (1995). *Looking into primary headship: A research based interpretation*. London: Falmer Press.

Southworth, G. (2005). Overview and conclusions. In M. J. Coles & G. Southworth (Eds.), *Developing leadership: Creating the schools of tomorrow* (pp. 158–173). Buckinghamshire: Open University Press.

Wong, K. (1998). Culture and moral leadership in education. *Peabody Journal of Education, 73*, 106–125.

Donald Malasa

Donald was born in Sasamungga village in Choiseul province. He attended Panarui Junior primary school and Sasamungga Senior primary school before moving on to Goldie college in Munda (Forms 1-5) and King George VI School (Form 6). He attended the University of the South Pacific in Suva where he graduated with a Bachelor of Education. He then taught mathematics and science at King George VI School. He took up a position as secondary mathematics curriculum development officer at the Curriculum Development Centre and was later promoted to Chief Curriculum Development Officer and then to Director. He was then appointed as Undersecretary for Education in the Ministry of Education and Human Resource Development. He completed a masters degree at the University of Waikato and is currently working as Acting Director of SICHE on secondment from MEHRD. Donald is married with five children and maintains an interest in watching soccer and rugby, reading, community work and gardening.

CHAPTER 5

Highly Effective School Principalship in the Solomon Islands

Collin Ruqebatu
Development Service Exchange, Solomon Islands

Introduction

There is an international consensus that highly successful schools are driven by highly successful principals (Beare, Caldwell, & Millikan, 1992; Calabrese & Zepeda, 1999; Day & Harris, 2001; Fullan, 2002; Millikan, 2002; Stoll & Fink, 1996). The statement holds true for many contexts, including the Solomon Islands. In line with international trends, Solomon Islands schools with highly effective principals have been successful. School principals are thus very significant players in ensuring that schools succeed (Bass, 1985; Bennett, Wise, & Woods, 2003; Caldwell, 2006; Day & Harris, 2001; Hord, 1997; Lambert, 2003; Southworth, 1999; West-Burnham, 2004).

I have a compelling personal interest in the area as I have been a serving principal in the Solomon Islands for the last two decades. My career as a school principal began when I was first appointed as the principal of Avuavu Provincial Secondary School in 1987. I started with very little idea of what this responsibility entailed. Over the years I began to explore what it means to be an effective school principal, and my interest was further enhanced by the leadership studies I pursued at the University of Waikato.

The vast amount of literature describing leadership experiences and studies by researchers in schools in many Western developed countries such as the United States, the United Kingdom, Australia and New Zealand intrigued me, and I began to wonder if some of the findings would be appropriate to help improve Solomon Islands school leadership, especially that of principals. Could the stories of how principals successfully lead and manage be adapted to different cultural and socioeconomic backgrounds in Solomon Islands schools? Could knowledge of how principals lead schools in developed countries be valid in developing countries such as ours? These questions fuelled my interest in pursuing research focusing on the elements of highly effective practices. An initial literature search indicated that very little research has been done on Solomon Islands school principalship.

National policy has contributed to the perceived current inadequacy of school leadership in the Solomon Islands. Over the years successive governments have failed to allocate resources for the positive development of school leadership. Now that the country is moving towards a federal system of government, it is even more urgent that a leadership package be developed to ensure our schools are better managed and led.

Unless current and future principals are made aware of the elements of highly effective principalship, they will continue to lead schools without informing their practice by reference to current literature and theory. Leading today's Solomon Islands schools without this knowledge is like a captain on a ship venturing out into the ocean without navigational equipment. The journey will depend on the captain's trial and error, and the ship will only reach its destination by sheer luck. From a long-term perspective, it is imperative that our schools are led by principals with appropriate knowledge, skills, vision and foresight, based on both professional experience and current leadership theory.

The practice of school leadership in the Solomon Islands schools today is problematic. Concerns are expressed by parents and the general public at the lack of efficiency and effectiveness (Malasa, 2007). For example, the problem of teachers' absenteeism stems from less-than-competent school leadership. I believed there was a need to interview current school principals about their perceptions of what constitutes highly effective principalship, a concept that is contestable because of its contextual specificity. I also wanted to encourage principals to identify and articulate current issues that prevent them from performing well so that these barriers can be addressed.

Research design

The study investigated the perceptions of six Honiara-based principals of community high schools (CHS), asking them about both the elements of highly effective principalship and issues that inhibit their effectiveness in their own context. The participants, five males and one female, all had more than seven years' experience as principals and had taught for lengthy periods before that. I chose a qualitative methodology to allow me to focus on the feelings, experiences and values of the participants, using an interpretive paradigm which allowed me to acknowledge the influence of political, economic and cultural forces on the way people think and behave.

I carried out semistructured interviews with all the participants and also made informal observations and consulted documents at the Ministry of Education and Human Resource Development (MEHRD) for the purpose of triangulating and confirming the findings from the interviews.

Perceptions of highly effective principalship in the Solomon Islands

The principals' perceptions were based on practical experience rather than any knowledge of current leadership theories. However, they expressed their views with confidence and clarity, and with a large degree of agreement. At times they appeared to conflate answers or answer questions obliquely. There were also interesting gaps in their answers. For example, they made no mention of important issues such as leading learning, leading for the future, preparing a nation for social and economic development and other macro issues. This implies a micromanagerial focus rather than an appreciation of the broader role of an educational leader.

Their answers were grounded in the values they believed a principal should exhibit, in turn based on Christian values. They saw highly effective principals as demonstrating commitment and dedication, competence, honesty, kindness, patience, listening, high interpersonal skills and good relationship building, role modelling, passion, vision, knowledge, persistence, punctuality, reliability and trustworthiness. A number of participants referred to ways of acting that could be considered virtuous but were also important leadership capacities. They sometimes had difficulty describing them, perhaps because they are somewhat intangible.

Links between traditional Solomon Islands leadership and principalship

The participants commented positively on the congruence of traditional Solomon Islands leadership practices with modern principalship. They agreed that the two types of leadership have a lot of similarities and can complement each other. The two styles of leadership emphasise similar leadership characteristics, including courage, good planning, strategic skills, knowledge and commitment. However, there were some areas where they found traditional leadership expectations could be an impediment to principalship.

School leadership values equality and fairness and does not entertain the cultural practice of "wantok", a system by which the traditional Solomon Islands leader is culturally obliged to serve his or her clan or tribe before others. Traditional leadership also incorporates sexist views that might see males being appointed as principals ahead of females who are more capable.

Another area where traditional leadership practices differ from those of modern principalship is the importance of time. In traditional Solomon Islands practice, time means little. Observers have noted that some school leaders are usually late in getting to school and leave earlier than the rest of the teachers. Here the principles of traditional leadership had infiltrated into modern schools and were becoming impediments to highly effective principalship.

Issues impeding effective principalship

The participants raised serious concerns about issues that prevent them (and principals in general) from developing higher levels of effectiveness as leaders of their schools. They gave strong indications that unless these issues were addressed earnestly and immediately, most school principals would continue to face an uphill battle in trying to lead their schools. Here is a brief summary of these issues:

- Lack of appropriate preprincipalship training or professional development: no principals are trained for their task.
- Lack of positive and timely responses from the MEHRD and local education authorities on important issues that affect the smooth and effective administration of schools throughout the country.
- Unfavourable conditions of service for the teaching profession, which have an impact on principals' ability to recruit and keep quality teachers. The participants believed that the MEHRD does not give sufficient money to finance all schools adequately. This means that schools lack money to buy curriculum materials, develop infrastructure and pursue more learner-centred programmes. This

is exacerbated for schools further away from the main centres as their budgets have to allocate greater amounts to transport. In addition, as more new schools open, the static national budgetary allocation or grant must be stretched even further.
- Insufficient inspectors: the participants claimed that the MEHRD and education authority officials fail to visit schools to carry out inspections or even visit schools as a way of reassuring principals, teachers and students, but instead are seen to be occupied in their centralised offices. The reasons for this are not clear to principals. It could be due to the same budgetary constraints imposed on schools, bureaucratic requirements for submitting to central Ministry offices or some other reason. Regrettably there was a feeling among some of the participants that it could involve matters of quality and professional ability. This perception has the potential to be detrimental to the entire system.

Discussion and significance of the findings

It is noteworthy that the views expressed by the participants were a function of personal experiences, without any theory-driven basis for their statements. All participants admitted they did not have significant knowledge of current educational leadership theory. They believed that the essence of effective leadership is dedication and commitment. Spending time, thought and energy on the school's environment, programmes and activities should, in the long term, bring about continuing levels of school success. However, it is significant that many school leaders in the Solomon Islands still need to display this commitment and dedication. This view was mooted by the participants and is supported in the literature (Malasa, 2007; Sikua, 2002). The participants also suggested that leading with Christian values enhanced the effectiveness of school leadership, and that those principals who demonstrated Christian values and morals and behaved spiritually were highly regarded by the school community.

Professional relationships

Participants perceived that it was important for principals to develop warm, cordial working relationships with higher authorities, such as MEHRD officials and the school's controlling authorities. This perception is in line with current literature on culture building. Robertson (2005) points out that leadership is about relationships, but that it is also highly political, which occasionally bedevils the practice. But good relationships can enhance quality learning and effective practice.

Individual qualities of a leader

The "big man" in a traditional Melanesian society was regarded as a born leader. (This would fall within the ambit of trait theory, as described in the literature.) The talents and attributes these leaders possessed set them apart from their followers. The traditional Solomon Islands leader gained the respect of society by working hard for it with spiritual, ethical and personal commitment and dedication. The same qualities are valued and respected in the current Solomon Islands school system. School communities respect the school principal who displays the qualities of a born leader. Some of these qualities include quality decision making, being ethical, humble, respectful, visionary and truthful. This is endorsed by Sanga and Walker (2005). School principals need to earn the trust of their school communities by displaying authentic school leadership. The participants also believed that a principal must be visionary, and able to lead the school with foresight and creativity. This view is supported by Hargreaves (1997), Kedian (2006), Robertson (1996) and Walter-Thomas and Di Paola (2003).

Although current literature leans more towards a shared, collaborative and constructivist leadership approach, some authors (Bass, 1998; Blasé & Blasé, 2004; Robertson, 1995) note that this type of "big man" concept of leadership is still important. In the case of the

Solomon Islands, the participants perceived that schools need more of this leadership style. They believed that principals who display these leadership qualities are more effective than those who do not in leading their schools. While there is an indigenous explanation for this, as implied above, there is an equally compelling argument that these leadership capacities could be developed by requiring principals to engage in a professional learning programme for leadership development.

A further aspect of leadership is courage. The participants saw this manifesting itself as a willingness to experiment and take professional risks in their schools. Principals must not be afraid to take academic risks in altering school programmes to enhance quality learning. Schools in the Solomon Islands need more school principals to be academic risk takers if they are to sustain excellence and develop a transformational ethic. Principals also need to take part in their school programmes more. The literature suggests that those who do so seem to enjoy their work, establish good relationships with staff and students and are more progressive (Caldwell, 2006; Glanz, 2006; Schumaker & Sommers, 2001; Sigford, 2006; Tomlinson, 2004).

Participants also noted that schools with principals who have appropriate communication skills and who encourage consultation benefit more from donor agencies and other providers than schools whose leaders do not display these skills. They were quick to point out that this could make a substantial difference to a school.

Managing, leading and becoming knowledgeable

One participant stated that "highly effective principals must know they are managers and they are leaders". Most of the participants seemed not to understand that leading and managing are not the same thing. Theorists encountered in the literature tend to make a clear distinction between leadership and management. Management covers routine tasks, while leadership involves taking the institution from point A to point B (Duignan, 1988; Kedian, 2006; Robertson, 1995; Sergiovanni, 1991. The lack of principals' access to literature and theory is likely to be the cause of participants lacking knowledge of the distinctions between leadership, management and administration.

Being knowledgeable was perceived by three participants to be an element of highly effective principalship. They stated that all principals—whether newly appointed or currently in the system—should complete leadership training, graduate with sound academic knowledge and continue to update themselves with recent information on different approaches to school leadership. Current literature emphasises that being knowledgeable should include reflectivity. This means that Solomon Islands principals need to reflect critically on what they have accomplished for their schools, and check where they are at and where they will take the school (Robertson, 1995). Principals also need to make time to assess their own performance, stop, look back and check their performances so far. By doing this they can evaluate their successes and shortfalls, find out why the shortfalls occurred and set a new bearing for the next part of the school's journey. Critical reflection is an essential part of leadership practice (Court, 1994; Duignan, 1988; Giddens, 1993; Kedian, 2006; Purkey & Smith, 1985; Robertson, 1996; Sigford, 2006).

Leading as role modelling

All participants regarded role modelling as the most highly effective way of leading schools. They said that actions speak louder than words. This is in line with the literature (Bennett et al., 2003; Blackmore, 2002; Blasé & Blasé, 2004; Gibson, 2005; Lambert, 2003; Southworth, 1999; Strike, 2007; West-Burnham, 2004). Importantly, however, none of them mentioned the notion of modelling learning. Arguably, the modelling needs to progress beyond the personal to the more professional aspects of teaching and learning.

Another aspect of role modelling relates to upholding the professional code of conduct for teachers, as laid out in Chapter 10 of the *Solomon Islands Teaching Service Handbook*. This document highlights the key commitments, professional responsibilities and ethical principles by which all school principals and teachers are expected to abide (MEHRD, 2007). The participants strongly believed that it was vital for a principal to display ethical leadership because it would motivate staff to perform over and above their normal duties. An ethical approach would ensure that principals and teachers serve the welfare of the school and transform learning for students. It would also ensure that principals adhere to expectations such as punctuality, attendance and participation. The literature consulted held similar views. Importantly, however, one of the participants pointed out that the professional code of conduct was extremely brief and potentially somewhat ambiguous. With no other training or education about the issues, educators could adopt a rather literal view of the code, resulting in principals or teachers taking advantage of this lack of clarity to get away with lack of professionalism.

Not all schools visited as part of the study evidenced explicit understanding and interpretation of ethical conduct and appropriate work ethic. The lack of work ethic can also be noticed in education authorities and the MEHRD. Participants agreed that if the MEHRD re-emphasised the notion of a work ethic in the education system of the country it would be a big step in the right direction.

Issues that impede highly effective principalship

The participants were adamant that lack of initial principal training has posed enormous challenges in the past and remains the biggest barrier to effective principalship. New principals are appointed to their schools without any induction or briefing on what their new roles and responsibilities will entail. In the past, this has resulted in a number of the appointees leaving the service when confronted by situations that were beyond their capability to understand and resolve. MEHRD reports have also identified that inadequate preparation for newly appointed principals has led to poor and unsuccessful leadership and management of schools in the past (MEHRD, 2005). Participants suggested that controlling authorities and the MEHRD should give principals the attention they need, provide the necessary support services and assist principals to lead their schools to success. The Solomon Islands MEHRD is fully aware of this issue (MEHRD, 2005), and the initiatives proposed in the Ministry's *Strategic Plan (2004–2006)* and *Education Corporate Plan (2006–2008)* are aimed at solving this. However, it appears that little has changed at a practical level.

Participant principals shared many examples of their experiences when timely responses were not forthcoming from the MEHRD or various education authorities. The requested responses ranged from higher order policy matters, to lower order, but equally important, administrative matters. For example, during the time I was carrying out field work in Honiara in June and July 2007, there were approximately 220 newly appointed teachers who had not received their first salary payments, even though they had been teaching for more than six months. This slowness by the MEHRD and education authorities hampered the work of the principals and affected the classroom teachers adversely. The participants noted also that in most cases of delay, teachers blame the school principal. The education authorities or the MEHRD usually resort to bureaucratic bluster. As a result, the reality is that principals are forced to devote disproportionately large amounts of time to resolving sometimes trivial administrative blunders and inefficiencies. It is important to note, also, that the views expressed here were made by urban principals in Honiara, whose schools are close to the MEHRD and the education authority. For rural schools the problem of delays by officials and authorities would be far more substantial. These issues cause much unnecessary frustration and stress for principals and their teachers.

Compared to other professional occupations in the Solomon Islands, teachers are lowly paid. For the past 20 years teachers have been paid less than their counterparts with the same qualifications in other government ministries and the private sector. For example, they receive no noncash benefits or holiday pay, which all other public servants receive. For some years teachers have been negotiating for better conditions of service, but with little or no success. This culminated in June 2007 in a two-week strike, based on the argument that the Government appeared not to be listening to their requests since there had been no observable improvements in their conditions of service. The dissatisfaction caused by these conditions is bad for morale and makes the task of principals more difficult.

Insufficient financial assistance from the Government and education authorities was a key issue for the participants. This, combined with delays in payment, causes difficulties for schools because they are unable to pay for all the resources they need. However, during the observation phase of the study I observed that schools that could raise funds in addition to the official school grants were very successful and seemed not to have financial problems. In the past, parents and school communities have shown willingness and enthusiasm in raising funds for the school when the principal showed openness, transparency and accountability. This may be the route for all Solomon Islands schools to follow, even though it appears to absolve the Ministry from its responsibility to fund schools appropriately.

Failure by the MEHRD and various education authority officials to undertake school visits for the purposes of conducting inspections and appraisals of teachers' performance for confirmation of appointment and promotions was seen as a serious impediment to quality by the participants. They raised concerns that the MEHRD and education authorities usually fail to follow up complaints made by the public and seem to show little interest in what individual principals are doing in their schools. Incidental information received during this study indicated that the MEHRD had never conducted teacher or principal appraisals throughout the country. Consequently, formal data regarding the effectiveness and performance levels of most teachers and all principals are nonexistent. This is a very serious concern, which requires a joint solution. There are a number of options for the Government to improve the current impasse of the Inspectorate Division. This is not the place to pursue that issue however.

Finally, I observed that most school principals are working in isolation. There is no established mechanism for principals to have the opportunity to share their successes and concerns. A network system should be in place for principals in different geographical areas to establish an avenue whereby they have the opportunity to discuss their professional activities and develop critical learning groups and critical friendships. Although this is an activity that could be initiated by principals, an outside catalyst is often important in the establishment phase.

The data gathered from the participants have provided a deep insight into the views of serving principals regarding effective principalship. But as in any research project using qualitative data-gathering strategies, the silences in the data are also important. There are omissions in areas where I would have anticipated from the literature that principals would offer information and opinion. For example, none saw their school as a social agent in the community or felt that the school should run parallel to community practice so that students will not be out of touch with their community when they leave school. Nor were they offered community courses. Another silence was the lack of reference to the extreme gender imbalance among school principals, among whom only 2.8 percent are female.

Conclusion

The research project described in this chapter set out to explore, expose and describe participating principals' views of highly effective principalship and identify impediments to it. It was one of the first research studies to investigate this topic. The results are unique to the Solomon Islands school context, but there was some correlation with current international literature on school leadership.

The study provides important information for the Solomon Islands MEHRD and various educational authorities by clarifying principals' concerns. It could be used as a contribution to the development of a strategic leadership training programme for the country. School principals could also use the study to support their own leadership journeys. Based on the findings, I conclude that principals need to be helped to develop a broader conception of the notion of "effective principalship" and contextually specific strategies for leading schools effectively. They need to develop their understanding of current leadership theories and a firm, theoretically sound basis for their leadership practices.

The development of a substantial work on the philosophy of educational leadership, focusing on effective educational leadership and principalship in the Solomon Islands, is critical to the ongoing national strategy and student wellbeing. *Apem Moa: Solomon Islands Leadership* (Sanga & Walker, 2005) is an important foundation and needs to be built on. Those in decision-making positions in the Solomon Islands also need to think seriously about generating a national educational leadership strategy, including effective principalship training strategies. This will benefit the children of the Solomon Islands. Their high performance depends on how successfully the schools run their programmes. The available literature suggests that successful schools develop highly motivated and enthusiastic teachers, who in turn are led by highly effective principals. It is crucial that the Government allocates time, money and energy to ensure the development of highly effective leaders in the country's schools.

References

Bass, B. (1985). *Leadership and performance beyond expectation*. New York: Free Press.

Bass, B. (1998). *Transformational leadership: Industrial, military and educational impact*. Mahwah, NJ: Lawrence Erlbaum.

Beare, H., Caldwell B., & Millikan, R. (1992). *Creating an excellent school*. London: Routledge.

Bennett, N., Wise, C., & Woods, P. (Eds.). (2003). *Distributed leadership*. Birmingham: National College for School Leadership.

Blackmore, J. (2002). Leadership for socially just schooling: More substance and less style in high-risk, low-trust times? *Journal of School Leadership, 112*, 198–222.

Blasé, J., & Blasé, J. (2004). *Handbook of instructional leadership: How successful principals promote teaching and learning* (2nd ed.). Thousand Oaks, CA: Sage.

Calabrese, R., & Zepeda, S. (1999). Decision-making assessment: Improving principal performance. *International Journal of Educational Management, 13*(1), 6–13.

Caldwell, B. (2006). *Re-imagining educational leadership*. Camberwell, VIC: ACER Press.

Court, M. (1994). *Women transforming leadership*. Palmerston North: Massey University ERDC Press.

Day, C., & Harris, A. (2001). *Effective school leadership*. Retrieved 13 December 2007, from http://www.ncsl.org.uk/mediastore/image2/kpool-evidenceday/pdf

Duignan, P. (1988). Reflective management: The key to quality leadership. *International Journal of Educational Management, 2*(2), 3–12.

Fullan, M. (2002). *The change leader*. Retrieved 12 December 2007, from http://www.cdl.org/resources

Gibson, A. (2005). The role of the principal in leadership in teaching and learning. *New Zealand Journal of Educational Leadership, 20*(1), 65–78.

Giddens, A. (1993). *New rules of sociological methods* (2nd ed.). Cambridge: Polity Press.

Glanz, J. (2006). *What every principal should know about collaborative leadership*. Thousand Oaks, CA: Corwin Press.

Hargreaves, A. (1997). Rethinking educational change: Going deeper and wider in the quest for success. In A. Hargreaves (Ed.). *Rethinking educational change with heart and mind: ASCD yearbook* (pp. 1–26). Retrieved 7 October 2006, from http://www.ascd.org

Hord, S. (1997). Professional learning communities: What are they and why are they important? *Issues About Change, 6*(1). Retrieved from http://www.sedl.org/change/issues/issues61.html

Kedian, J. (2006). *Organisational development* [lecture notes]. University of Waikato, Hamilton.

Lambert, L. (2003). Leadership capacity for lasting reform. *Educational Leadership, 62*(5), 62–65.

Malasa, D. (2007). *Effective school leadership: An exploration of the issues inhibiting the effectiveness of school leadership in Solomon Islands secondary schools.* Unpublished master's thesis, University of Waikato, Hamilton.

MEHRD. (2005). *2004 Annual report*. Honiara: Author.

MEHRD. (2007). *Solomon Islands teaching service handbook*. Honiara: Author.

Millikan, J. (2002). Qualifying for leadership or control masquerading as enlightenment? *International Journal of Public Sector Management, 15*(4), 281–295.

Purkey, S., & Smith, M. (1985). School reform: The district policy implications of the effective schools literature. *Elementary School Journal, 85*(3), 353–389.

Robertson, J. (1995). *Theories of leadership: Educational leadership: Issues and perspectives* [lecture notes]. University of Waikato, Hamilton.

Robertson, J. (1996). *Are we in the right jungle? Professional partners help New Zealand principals refocus on educational leadership* [lecture notes]. University of Waikato, Hamilton.

Robertson, J. (2005). *Coaching leadership: Building educational leadership capacity through coaching partnerships*. Wellington: NZCER Press.

Sanga, K., & Walker, K. (2005). *Apem moa: Solomon Islands leadership*. Wellington: He Parekereke, Victoria University of Wellington.

Schumaker, D., & Sommers, W. (2001). *Being a successful principal: Riding the wave of change without drowning*. Thousand Oaks, CA: Corwin Press.

Sergiovanni, T. (1991). *The principalship: A reflective practice perspective* (2nd ed.). Needham Heights, MA: Allyn & Bacon.

Sigford, J. (2006). *The effective school leader's guide to management*. Thousand Oaks, CA: Corwin Press.

Sikua, D. (2002). *The decentralisation of education in a developing country: A case of community high schools in the Solomon Islands*. Unpublished PhD thesis, University of Waikato, Hamilton.

Southworth, G. (1999). *Lessons for successful leadership in small schools*. Reading: University of Reading, School of Education.

Stoll, L. , & Fink, D. (1996). *Changing our schools: Linking school effectiveness and school improvement*. Buckinghamshire: Open University Press.

Strike, K. (2007). *Ethical leadership in schools: Creating community in an environment of accountability*. Thousand Oaks, CA: Corwin Press.

Tomlinson, H. (2004). *Educational leadership: Personal growth for professional development*. London: Sage.

Walter-Thomas, C., & Di Paola, M. (2003). What instructional leaders need to know about special education. In W. Owings & L. Kaplan (Eds.), *Best practices, best thinking, and emerging issues in school leadership* (pp. 123–136). Thousand Oaks, CA: Corwin Press.

West-Burnham, J. (2004). *Leadership development and personal effectiveness*. Retrieved from http://www/ncsl.org.uk/media/759/58/leadership-development-and-personal-effectiveness.pdf

Collin Ruqabatu

Collin is one of nine children. He is from the island of Choiseul in the northern part of the Solomon Islands. He did his primary schooling in Choiseul and the Western Province before attending St Joseph's Catholic Secondary school on Guadalcanal. Collin trained as a secondary teacher at the Solomon Islands Teachers College (now the Solomon Islands College of Higher Education). After a number of years of teaching throughout the Solomon Islands Collin was appointed as principal of Bishop Epalle Catholic School in Honiara. In 2006 he studied at the University of Waikato for a Master of Educational Leadership degree, graduating in 2009. Collin is married with two children. He is currently the General Secretary of the Development Services Exchange, the national umbrella body for nongovernment organisations in the Solomon Islands. Collin maintains an active interest in education and is very involved in the Catholic church.

CHAPTER 6
Seen But Not Heard: The Educational Leadership Experiences of Women Leaders in Solomon Islands Secondary Schools

Shalom Akao
New Zealand High Commission, Honiara, Solomon Islands

Introduction

In my profile for a school magazine in sixth grade, I wrote that my ambition was "To become the first woman Prime Minister of Solomon Islands". That was a childhood dream, but my interest in women and leadership had already begun. Throughout my high school days and my year at the Solomon Islands College of Higher Education (SICHE), I stood up for women's issues. In classroom debates about women as leaders I argued for women to be included, especially in Parliament. My interest in women's issues was reinforced when I went to New Zealand to study. One of the courses that really opened my eyes was Women in Society. I started to question many of the things I had taken for granted in relation to being a woman.

After completing my studies I came back to the Solomon Islands and taught as a secondary school teacher. It was then I started to notice that the majority of principals were men. I also observed that although women teachers held positions of responsibility, they played a minor role and at times were left out of the decision-making process. This started to raise questions for me. In my postgraduate study I was introduced to the complex world of educational leadership and realised that women can play a significant role as leaders. Reflecting on leadership in Solomon Islands secondary schools, I felt women's experiences were missing and I wondered why. I felt the need to undertake research to learn from other Solomon Islands women what they have to share about their leadership experiences in secondary schools, and what they believe to be the challenges and constraints that have had an impact on their leadership roles. The research reported in this chapter provides an avenue to give women a voice.

In Solomon Islands secondary schools nearly all the educational administration and leadership positions—such as principals, deputy principals and heads of departments—are filled by men (MEHRD, 2006). A survey conducted in 2006 by the Ministry of Education and Human Resources Development (MEHRD) showed that only 27.8 percent of all secondary teachers were women. Of the 103 secondary school principals, only three (2.9 percent) were female (MEHRD, 2006). Such statistics illustrate that women are grossly underrepresented as secondary teachers and school leaders. The issue this raises is one of social injustice within educational leadership with regard to gender inequality. In addition, although much research has been carried out in developed and developing countries, very little has come from Melanesian countries. We know very little about women and educational leadership in Melanesia, with the exception of work by Kilavanwa (2004), Strachan (2002) and Strachan, Saunders, Jimmy, and Lapi (2007). In view of this, the current study is underpinned by the following question: What are the leadership experiences of women educational leaders in Solomon Islands secondary schools?

Research methodology and process

My research used a qualitative methodology set within a feminist research paradigm. Using a feminist lens was important, because all the participants were women. They came from different islands, with unique customs and cultures that had shaped their lives and experiences. I wanted to put these women at the centre of the inquiry and allow them to voice their views and opinions freely, so that we can better understand their leadership experiences from their own perspectives.

As a Solomon Islands woman I was an insider in this study. Because I am of the culture, the women felt free to share their experiences because they knew that I had had similar experiences. Therefore, my personal "insider status should not be seen as a dangerous bias but a necessary prerequisite condition for the sharing of intimate information" (Strachan, 1993, p. 76). This built status trust among the participants. At this point of my research journey I do not have the courage to identify myself as a feminist because I come from a society that snubs anyone who tries to go against the cultural norms. Regardless, as a woman interested in women's issues and in working for social justice, I join with other women leaders as partners to address some common but very sensitive issues such as representation, equality, voice, emancipation and empowerment (Cohen, Manion, & Morrison, 2000).

Initially I set out to include women who were current principals and deputy principals of secondary schools in the Solomon Islands. Time constraints and unreliable travel services prevented me from going to provinces other than Guadalcanal. Invitation letters were sent to eight women, three of whom were principals and five deputy principals. I was able to make contact with the five deputy principals, who were all willing to participate. Unfortunately, the involvement of the three principals did not eventuate. Three replacements, all heads of departments, were found. I interviewed each woman face to face for approximately an hour in her school, a place both convenient and accessible for her.

All eight interviews were conducted in pidgin (the *lingua franca* of the Solomon Islands) and taperecorded, except for one, with a woman who did not wish to be taperecorded. Her wishes were respected, and I had the daunting task of trying to capture all the important things she was saying by hand. Interview notes were also kept for the other women who had agreed to be taperecorded so that aspects of the interview the taperecorder could not capture, such as expressions on the women's faces, were noted down.

Leadership experiences of the women in the study

Getting appointed

None of the women interviewed had problems gaining leadership positions in their schools. In other words, the findings of this study do not support previous research on the selection of leaders for schools, which notes the huge influence that male gatekeepers have in the selection process, tending to disadvantage women (Blackmore, 1993, 1999; Blackmore, Thomson, & Barty, 2006; Coleman, 2002, 2005; Evetts, 1994; Hall, 1996). All the women commented that the positions they filled were never advertised; they were appointed because they had performed their assigned duties well. Although there are formal selection procedures to select leaders into schools, these procedures were not followed. A possible explanation for this is that if a position is vacant for a long time it needs to be filled quickly. Perhaps the principals and education authorities did not want the work involved in looking for a replacement. Maybe they chose the next available candidate—one who was already in the school or in close proximity to it.

Brooking (2005) notes that women are selected into leadership positions because a suitable male candidate has not applied, so a woman is picked to fill the post. A point to consider, too, is that male teachers may not want to be deputy principals. They may not want to follow someone else's orders, even if it is from a male colleague, but instead prefer to be the person giving the orders. This may be attributed to how they were raised: to be men and give orders, rather than take them.

This lack of transparency in the selection process may have enabled these women to be appointed to leadership positions, but not following procedure could make it difficult for other women to gain such positions. On the one hand, it is encouraging that this selection process has allowed women to be placed into school leadership roles. On the other hand, questions need to be raised about whether the education authorities are really doing their job and how this affects their role of providing quality education for the students of the Solomon Islands. Blackmore (1989) has argued that we should not merely be looking to increase the number of women in educational leadership, but should "go beyond the numbers game" (p. 95).

In the context of the Solomon Islands, it is imperative that there be more women in leadership positions, so that their visibility will encourage other women to think of themselves as leaders. Seeing more women in leadership positions may motivate and inspire more women to take up leadership positions, which may start to address women's underrepresentation in leadership positions in education.

Feeling a lack of confidence

This study found that the women leaders had low self-confidence and self-esteem, which inhibited them in their leadership role. Some even felt guilty about their success:

> When I was told that I would be head of department I felt bad. This was because the other teacher, a man, had been teaching for more

than 10 years and I felt that because he had been teaching for longer than me he should have been given that post. I think I feel like this because of the mentality that men should be leaders.

This lack of confidence was not because they could not do their job. However, for six out of the eight women, this was their first leadership role. Shakeshaft (1987) and Cubillo and Brown (2003) found that women's so-called lack of confidence has more to do with unfamiliarity with the territory than a lack of faith in their own abilities. In her ground-breaking research, Shakeshaft highlighted the fact that this lack of confidence is measured and defined by male standards, whereby:

> Women have self-confidence in areas in which they have experience (private sphere functions), whereas men have self-confidence in areas in which they have been allowed to participate (public sphere functions). Therefore low self-confidence might be viewed then, as a product of a system that keeps women separated from experiences that would help build confidence in the public sphere. (1987, p. 84)

Coleman (2002, 2005) notes that this lack of confidence is often linked to the fact that women are in an environment where leaders are expected to be male.

The women attributed their lack of confidence to the influence of their cultural socialisation patterns. From an early age, women in the Solomon Islands learn and practise scripts that are different from those of men (Cubillo & Brown, 2003; Kilavanwa, 2004). They are taught to respect and take care of their brothers and husbands, and not to answer back to male relatives but do as they are told (Pollard, 2000; Vaa, 2006). The women in this study noted that they felt ashamed when they had to tell male teachers what to do because culturally it is not acceptable for a woman to do that. This may hinder women's ability to do their job. There may be delays in the completion of assigned tasks, and in some instances male teachers may not do what they have been asked to do by women leaders. This finding reinforces the point Pollard (2000) raises about the socialisation of girls, whereby indirectly "girls are taught to accept the traditional roles of subordination, and subservience to males" (p. 4).

A possible explanation is that these women are in a society where even though changes have occurred in nearly all aspects of the society, hegemonic traditions and culture are upheld (Cubillo & Brown, 2003). Men can adapt to changes in society, but women are expected to continue to hold on to traditional stereotypical roles such as housekeeping and child-raising (Aladejana & Aladejana, 2005; Cubillo & Brown, 2003; Hasibuan-Sedyono, 1998; Oplatka, 2006; Pollard, 2000; Strachan et al., 2007; Vaa, 2006). So when women are in positions of leadership, they are challenged. Women in these situations need a place to share their leadership experiences with others who are experiencing similar circumstances.

Although this is a possible solution, some women may not see the importance of this or may not feel comfortable joining such a group. This may be because some people may not look too kindly on such initiatives because of stereotypical attitudes, such as women using such groups to gossip about others. To avoid this, at the very first stage, ground rules and guidelines need to be set, by which those who wish to join such groups must abide. Another suggestion is that an experienced facilitator be brought in to facilitate such initiatives.

Balancing work and family

In this study the participants felt that the roles ascribed to women in the domestic sphere affected their leadership, and that juggling family responsibilities at home contributed to their not being able to carry out their job at school effectively. When there is a crisis at home, it is taken for granted that women will leave what they are doing to resolve the matter. An example is when children are sick: it is expected that mothers are responsible for taking them to the doctor. This finding is consistent with other research, which found that the dual role that women play—that of leader and wife—can be difficult (Aladejana & Aladejana, 2005; Coleman, Haiyan, & Yanping, 1998; Moorosi, 2007). This is more so for women in Melanesia. As Kilavanwa (2004) notes, "playing double roles at home and at work can be exhausting and adds pressure on them but they have to somehow manage it because they have to do it every day" (p. 65).

Strachan (2007) highlights the fact that teaching is a respected and sought-after career option for both men and women in Melanesia because opportunities for paid employment are very limited. Therefore, while women in developed countries like New Zealand (Strachan, 1991) and Great Britain (Evetts, 1994) can choose to take time out from their career to raise their children, Melanesian women cannot. Although their traditional roles at home are still the same, the replacement of the traditional economic system with a new one, which is based on cash, has changed women's roles. With education and employment taking women away from home, instead of cultivating their own food they now purchase food with cash (Pollard, 2000). This change, combined with the limited opportunities for paid employment, means women may not be able to take time out to raise their children but have to manage this dual role as best they can. Where both parents are working, it is women who may have to take time off from their jobs. When this happens, it has an impact on their earnings.

Earlier studies in other developing nations such as Indonesia (Hasibuan-Sedyono, 1998) and Trinidad and Tobago (Morris, 1998) have shown contrasting findings. In these countries it has been found that family responsibilities had not impeded women's careers because they had spouses who supported them as well as support from extended family networks. Although all the women in this study said that their husbands supported them, this finding needs to be interpreted with caution, because although the women noted their husbands' support in relation to their leadership roles, they did not mention whether this support is also shown in the home with regard to the men helping them with the domestic chores such as cooking, cleaning and washing. For these women, combining a career and family was problematic.

Violence against women

Although the women in this study had support from their husbands, they noted that some other women might not. Lack of support from husbands may contribute to the underrepresentation of women in leadership roles in schools. Women may be asked to fill a leadership position, but their husbands do not allow them to accept such offers. This may be explained by the fact that because their culture sees men as being superior, this has resulted in limitations on women's freedoms, movement, opportunities and choices. Some women face strong opposition from men, which results in violence (Kilavanwa, 2004). Men may feel insecure (Amnesty International, 2004; Brouwer, Harris, & Tanaka, 1998; Kilavanwa, 2004) about having women as the breadwinners, so they may limit women's opportunities. Violence against women may be attributable to the socialisation process in the Solomon Islands, whereby men are taught to be outspoken, aggressive, strong and authoritative, and women are conditioned to be submissive and silent (Pollard, 2000), so they do not retaliate when they are hit by their brothers or husbands. Vaa (2006) shares similar sentiments, but also highlights the role of Christianity with regard to this violence. This finding reinforces observations by Strachan (2007), who notes that violence against women has limited women's opportunities for participating in leadership.

How to address domestic violence is a significant issue. Violence against women is prevalent in Melanesian societies today (Amnesty International, 2004; Garap, 2004; Kilavanwa, 2004; Vaa, 2006). While a start has been made by the island nations with the widely ratified Convention on Elimination of All Forms of Discrimination

Against Women (CEDAW), there is still a long way to go. Only full implementation of CEDAW will ensure this issue is addressed so that women's potential is fully tapped (Vaa, 2006), and women's access to and participation in leadership is accepted by the predominantly male societies.

Discrimination

The findings of this study indicate that there were both overt and covert discrimination against the women, who faced discriminatory and sexist attitudes from members of society—especially from the men in their schools—because of being female. One woman, newly appointed as a deputy principal, had to listen to her male principal announce to a meeting of all staff that he did not want a woman deputy. Another reported that at one school the male teachers had their rent paid but the females did not because it was expected that their husbands should pay. These findings are consistent with other research (Bell & Chase, 1993; Coleman, 1996, 2002, 2005; Schmuck & Schubert, 1995; Shakeshaft, 1987; Skrla, Reyes, & Scheurich, 2000; Strachan, 1991) and corroborate much of the previous research on women and educational leadership. For example, Coleman (2002) found that women were strongly aware of the resentment felt by men in dealing with female leaders, and that gender stereotypes in educational leadership centre on the unthinking belief that there is a natural order, portrayed by male leadership and female subordination.

There is no gender equity policy in education in the Solomon Islands. The Solomon Islands Government passed the National Women's Policy in 1998, but it was never fully implemented. In 2009 the policy was reviewed and updated to make it more relevant, and from the lessons learnt a national action plan has been formulated to ensure the policy is implemented and monitored. Regardless, this policy needs to be adapted to the education sector. Maybe when there is a gender equity policy in education we may start to see the underrepresentation of women in leadership positions being addressed, as well as attending to other women's issues.

Lack of initial preparation, leadership training and ongoing professional learning

None of the women in the study were given initial leadership or management training before taking up a leadership role, nor any ongoing professional support. This is true of many countries—both developed and developing. There are similarities between this study and those of Malasa (2007) for the Solomon Islands, Puamu (1998) in Fiji, Kelep-Malpo (2003) for Papua New Guinea and other developing countries like Botswana (Pheko, 2008), where the participants also identified lack of training as one of the inhibiting factors for their leadership in the schools. In the Solomon Islands, parents and members of the school communities (MEHRD, 2004, 2005) have also highlighted this issue. Malasa (2007) points out that lack of initial preparation poses an enormous challenge to the growth and development of the leadership capacity of principals, teachers and students, as well as to the whole school system in the Solomon Islands.

This lack of initial leadership training may have a particular impact on the aspirations of women. My study found that women did not have the same access to limited leadership and management training as men. It seems possible that this is due to the androcentric nature of the organisations where these women work, in systems that privilege men. Leadership positions in the MEHRD, the education authorities and also the majority of schools are predominantly held by men, who may choose only men to attend the available courses. This may mean that women are excluded from participating in any organised leadership development. Programmes should be initiated to offer women the opportunity to learn skills that will assist them as leaders and motivate and inspire them to take on leadership roles.

Lack of consultation in the decision-making process

The women in this study reported a lack of consultation in school decision-making processes between women leaders and their male principals:

> [In] other areas like finance there are times that I do not have any say at all ... If they bring a cheque for me to sign but I question them about what the cheque is for, they will take it to another signatory.

A possible explanation for this can be found in the culture. As Strachan et al. (2007) note, "culture significantly affects females' ability to participate in education and decision-making at all levels, including educational leadership" (p. 40). This lack of consultation can be attributed to cultural attitudes, such as that women's place is in the home and that only men should take part in decision making (Cox & Aitsi, 1988; Strachan, 2007; Tuivaga, 1988). This may explain why some male principals did not want to include women in the decision making.

Another possible explanation for the lack of consultation is that schools in the Solomon Islands are still organised in bureaucratic and hierarchical ways, whereby overall authority is accorded to the principal (Blackmore, 1989). This overall authority may be misinterpreted by the principal to mean that they alone should make decisions, and so they do not discuss issues with those they work with, such as the deputy principals, heads of departments and the teachers in general. This may be seen as an abuse of power, although this issue also has to be looked at in relation to the leadership style of the principal. Moreover, it is possible that this type of attitude reflects a concept of having power over others, which Robertson (1996) argues is in conflict with current effective leadership theory, which emphasises community building and collaboration.

What can be done to facilitate women's leadership in Solomon Islands secondary schools?

Allowing women to lead in their own way

The findings of this study have shown that although the women had no leadership training prior to taking their leadership positions, they identified with the collaborative style of leadership. When asked what good leadership is, the phrases they used to describe this included team work, collaboration and participatory decision making, good management skills and relationship building with teachers, students and the larger community. These descriptions are consistent with a collaborative style of leadership, and this style of leadership is most strongly identified with women leaders (Blackmore, 2002; Coleman, 2002; Court, 1994, 2005; Evetts, 1994; Hall, 1993, 1996; Morris, 1998; Shakeshaft, 1987). Blackmore (2002) comments that women are seen as a new source of leadership talent because of their "caring and sharing propensities, their communicative and organizational skills and their capacity to listen and empathize with the needs of others" (p. 59).

The women's comments about leadership also highlight listening and helping others, and putting the needs of others before their own. This view of leadership is closely aligned with servant leadership (Narokobi, 1983; Pollard, 2006; Sanga & Walker, 2005), whereby leadership is about service, helping and supporting others. This view of leadership is similar to that expressed by women in Strachan et al.'s (2007) leadership programme in Vanuatu.

Although the women shared how they would like to lead, their stated responsibilities—as outlined in the *Solomon Islands Teaching Service Handbook* (MEHRD, 2007)—limit their capacities. As they indicated, their assigned responsibilities focus more on the management aspect of leadership, where great effort is put into planning and organising the daily operations of the school (Calabrese

& Zepeda, 1999; Duignan, 1989; Hoy & Miskel, 1991; Senge, 1990; Sigford, 2006). This suggests that the education system in the Solomon Islands still upholds the hierarchical and bureaucratic nature of the organisation, contrary to current leadership theories.

This finding has important implications for developing leadership training and ongoing professional learning. There is a need for leaders in Solomon Islands schools to distinguish between managerial, administrative and leadership activities. Understanding these distinctions will help them to understand and create strategies to lead highly effective learning in their schools rather than retreating into the relative comfort of efficient administration. As Robertson (1996) points out:

> Principals must first and foremost think of their role as one of educational leadership ... Principals must strive to resist the forces of managerialism ... Principals need help in developing and articulating their educational vision so that they can use management techniques as tools ... management should be a means to an end. (para 1–4)

Providing access to education and professional development for women

Strachan (2007) has noted that addressing the underrepresentation of women in educational leadership positions begins with gaining access to education. Because girls are less able to access education, this creates a flow-on effect, which impedes the participation of women (Brouwer et al., 1998; Strachan, 2007) in educational leadership, and subsequently their access to leadership training. This finding supports Kilavanwa's (2004) study showing that women's access to educational leadership is restricted by the "sites of gender inequality (male bias), division of labour, and the restricted access to education and resources" (p. 24).

The MEHRD is fully aware of the need for initial leadership training and support (MEHRD, 2005) and has proposed initiatives in its *National Education Strategic Plan 2004–2006* and *Education Corporate Plan 2006–2008* aimed at addressing this issue. However,

Malasa (2007) has commented that the initiatives merely address the planning, financing and management of the schools, and very little is aimed at improving the leadership capacities of the principals. This suggests that leaders in schools are merely learning to be effective managers, which is not the same thing as leading (Robertson, 1995; Schein, 1985; Sergiovanni, 1992). Because of the hierarchical nature of the schools, this means the women in this study are forced to do rather than decide; to implement rather than to lead (Robertson, 1995; Schein, 1985; Sergiovanni, 1992).

There need to be professional development opportunities solely for women because, as already mentioned, women make up only 2.9 percent of the principals. Women deputy principals and heads of departments have more limited access to professional development. This may be due to the hierarchical nature of the school organisation, where authority is seen to be legitimately accorded to the principal, usually a male (Blackmore, 1989), who will usually have access to any such training. Other leaders, such as the deputy principal, heads of department and teachers are left out. Programmes should be initiated to offer women the opportunity to learn skills that will assist them as leaders and motivate and inspire them to take on leadership roles.

If there is to be leadership training solely for women leaders of the Solomon Islands, there should be a collaborative process between facilitators and participants (Saunders, 2005) so that women are empowered through the training. It is also vital that the programme is culturally appropriate (Strachan et al., 2007). For women in the Solomon Islands, any professional development programme created needs to take into consideration and acknowledge their diverse cultures, but at the same time stay true to the needs of the women. This leadership development process should not only be for women in schools, but also for women in other formal sectors and nonformal sectors of the community. The good news is that the current Solomon Islands Government has established a Women's Ministry, which is responsible for addressing women's issues. The

Government now realises that women's issues may not have received adequate attention and is serious about making changes to advance the status of women.

Acknowledging the influence of culture and gender on attitudes towards women leaders

A recurring theme that permeated this study is the influence of culture and gender on attitudes towards women leaders. Culture and gender are interwoven. The findings of this study have indicated that some men do not take kindly to women in leadership positions and behave negatively towards them:

> Our culture sees the status of women as being inferior and so in schools it is the same ... Even here in our school some of the decisions that our deputy makes the principal just overrides. Some of the things that she says or she assigns tasks to be done, no one takes it seriously. I feel it's because she is a woman.

There are similarities between the attitudes expressed by the participants in this study and those described by Coleman (2002), Hasibuan-Sedyono (1998) and Oplatka (2006). Hart (1995) also notes that when women ascend to leadership positions in schools, often those whom they are assigned to lead immediately form negative expectations on the basis of a past, less than satisfactory, experience with one woman in a position of power, or on the basis of cultural stereotypes about women leaders. However, as also noted by the participants, not all men have negative attitudes towards women, which a previous study by Coleman (2002) has also shown. The culture of the society and gender have both greatly influenced and affected the leadership experiences of the women leaders in this study, especially in relation to their self-confidence, family responsibilities and work life, including discriminatory attitudes towards them.

It is evident from this study that women's participation in educational leadership is not only affected by structural or personal barriers: equally important are social barriers in the form of cultural expectations. These expectations are in the form of of sex role stereotypes, and traditional and historical influences. Moorosi (2007) argues that:

> These factors are so deeply rooted within schools as organizations and the society at large. They are therefore regarded as normal and gender neutral because they have always been the order of the day, and because they are so deeply entrenched, they are difficult to eradicate. (p. 519)

She goes on to claim that any plans for change need first to identify the "gendered social practices both within schools and the society" (p. 519), and then find ways to tackle these issues as and when they occur so as to achieve broader and genuine gender equity. For this to be effective, everyone needs to be involved in trying to eradicate these inequalities.

The issues raised here are issues of social justice. The concept of social justice focuses on marginalised groups, which are those groups that are most often underserved and underrepresented (Dantley & Tillman, 2005. Leadership for social justice is about working for change wherever inequality is found (Strachan, 2006). In particular, it is "a deliberate intervention that challenges fundamental inequities that arise ... due to the inappropriate use of power by one group over another" (Furman & Shields, 2005, p. 123). While this may seem a daunting task, those of us who are concerned with social justice issues must work to find ways to bring about change, especially in the implementation. Without hard toil, women's issues will remain stagnant.

One good example is the Solomon Islands National Women's Policy. After a frustrating five-year history of rejection and procrastination, the National Women's Policy was finally passed through Parliament in 1998. Wallace (2000) notes that while there were clear guidelines for addressing gender inequality through the policy, the problem and level of commitment and support for their effective implementation remain. Moreover, this policy is not specifically related to the education sector, so there is still a lot of work needing to be done. As Strachan (2004) highlighted, "social justice work is hard work and it takes courage. It also never ends, it is an ongoing process, we never reach the goal but we are always working towards it" (p. 3).

Conclusion

The women in this study had not planned their careers, and were simply appointed to their positions of leadership without going through the proper process. They had no initial preparation and leadership training and no ongoing professional development. This affected the women's leadership in their schools. The study also showed that where leadership and management training were offered, women did not have the same access as men. Despite their lack of training, the women had clear ideas about their preferred styles of leadership, even though this differed greatly from their stated responsibilities. In general, therefore, it seems that women and their experiences in the Solomon Islands continue to be marginalised. Taken together, these results suggest that the influence of gender and society's culture greatly impede the efficiency and role satisfaction of women's leadership in secondary schools.

One of the more significant findings to emerge from this study is that discrimination against women is evident in the Solomon Islands. This is due in large part to the influence of traditional cultural practices and customs, which are patriarchal. The women also spoke about their lack of confidence, and the challenge of balancing family responsibilities and work in relation to their gender and culture, and how this had an impact on their educational leadership. These findings suggest that the marginalisation of women continues in the Solomon Islands through the discriminatory actions and attitudes shown towards women in leadership positions.

This study adds to a growing body of literature on the educational leadership experiences of women in developing countries—especially women in the Pacific region, and in particular in Melanesia. The findings add substantially to our understanding of the influence of social culture and the role it plays in sustaining male dominance, which has greatly affected the leadership experiences of women. The study has enhanced our understanding of the challenges that women in Melanesian society experience in educational leadership and will serve as a base for future studies. It is hoped that the key findings of this research may initiate positive steps towards changing this social injustice. The findings of this study will be useful for the MEHRD and the Ministry of Women, Youth and Children's Affairs in the Solomon Islands.

To bring about change in women's access to education and leadership positions, and to societal attitudes towards women in the Solomon Islands, will need a lot of hard work, commitment and dedication on the part of all women and men. I hope that the key findings of this research initiate positive steps towards changing this social injustice. The above-mentioned ministries must start work on a gender equity policy to address issues such as gender inequality in employment, and access to education and leadership for girls and women.

This is one solution, but the hard task will be in the implementation of such a policy. While waiting for such policy, the onus is on us, the women of the Solomon Islands. What can we do? I suggest that we start with our children. Encourage our daughters to go to school. Those of us who have been fortunate enough to attend tertiary education must disseminate the knowledge we have acquired and share our experiences with other women. Through this we may empower them to do the same. Needless to say, all women must unite and start to take a stand to fight against these injustices, because collectively we are stronger.

If Solomon Islands women are to fight for their rights, the starting point should be the strengths valued within the local community. Keeping the balance between culturally oppressive agendas and the good practices of the community will enable an outlook to the future that is holistic and achievable. Therefore, women in leadership roles should foster relationship mechanisms that combine Western and local values in order to enhance the quest to raise the status of women in the Solomon Islands.

References

Aladejana, F., & Aladejana, T. I. (2005). Leadership in education: The place of Nigerian women. *International Studies in Educational Administration, 33*(2), 69–75.

Amnesty International. (2004). *Solomon Islands women confronting violence*. Retrieved 30 April 2008, from http://web.amnesty.org/library/index/engasa430012004

Bell, C. S., & Chase, S. (1993). The underrepresentation of women in school leadership. In C. Marshall (Ed.), *The new politics of race and gender: The 1992 yearbook of the Politics of Education Association* (pp. 141–151). Washington: Falmer.

Blackmore, J. (1989). Educational leadership: A feminist critique and reconstruction. In J. Smyth (Ed.), *Critical perspectives on educational leadership* (pp. 93–129). New York: Falmer.

Blackmore, J. (1993). In the shadow of men: The historical construction of administration as a "masculinist" enterprise. In J. Blackmore & J. Kenway (Eds.), *Gender matters in educational administration policy* (pp. 27–48). London: Falmer.

Blackmore, J. (1999). *Troubling women: Feminism, leadership, and educational change*. Buckingham and Philadelphia: Open University Press.

Blackmore, J. (2002). Troubling women: The upsides and downsides of leadership and the new managerialism. In C. Reynolds (Ed.), *Women and school leadership: International perspectives* (pp. 49–69). Albany, NY: State University of New York Press.

Blackmore, J., Thomson, P., & Barty, K. (2006). Principal selection: Homosociobility, the search for security and the production of normalized principal identities. *Educational Management Administration & Leadership, 34*(3), 297–317.

Brooking, K. (2005). Boards of trustees' selection of primary principals in New Zealand. *Delta, 57*(1 & 2), 117–140.

Brouwer, E. C., Harris, B. M., & Tanaka, S. (1998). *Gender analysis in Papua New Guinea*. Washington: World Bank.

Calabrese, R. L., & Zepeda, S. J. (1999). Decision-making assessment: Improving principal performance. *International Journal of Educational Management, 13*(1), 6–13.

Cohen, L., Manion, L., & Morrison, K. (2000). *Research methods in education* (5th ed.). New York: Routledge.

Coleman, M. (1996). The management style of female headteachers. *Educational Management & Administration, 24*(2), 163–174.

Coleman, M. (2002). *Women as headteachers: Striking the balance.* Stoke-on-Trent, England: Trentham.

Coleman, M. (2005). Gender and secondary school leadership. *International Studies in Educational Administration, 33*(2), 3–20.

Coleman, M., Haiyan, Q., & Yanping, L. (1998). Women in educational management in China: Experience in Shaanxi Province. *Compare, 28*(2), 141–154.

Court, M. (1994). *Women transforming leadership.* Palmerston North: Massey University ERDC Press.

Court, M. (2005). Negotiating and reconstructing gendered leadership discourses. In J. Collard & C. Reynolds (Eds.), *Leadership, gender and culture in education. Male and female perspectives* (pp. 3–17). New York: Open University Press.

Cox, E., & Aitsi, L. (1988). Papua New Guinea. In T. Tongamoa (Ed.), *Pacific women: Roles and status of women in Pacific societies* (pp. 23–38). Suva: Institute of Pacific Studies of the University of the South Pacific.

Cubillo, L., & Brown, M. (2003). Women into educational leadership and management: International differences? *Journal of Educational Administration, 41*(3), 278–291.

Dantley, M. E., & Tillman, L. C. (2005). Social justice and moral transformative leadership. In C. Marshall & M. Olivia (Eds.), *Leadership for social justice: Making revolutions in education* (pp. 16–30). Boston: Pearson Education.

Duignan, P. A. (1989). Reflective management: The key to quality leadership. In C. Riches & C. Morgan (Eds.), *Human resources management in education* (pp. 74–90). Buckingham: The Open University Press.

Evetts, J. (1994). *Becoming a secondary headteacher.* London and New York: Cassell.

Furman, G. C., & Shields, C. M. (2005). How can educational leaders promote and support social justice and democratic community in schools? In W. A. Firestone & C. Riehl (Eds.), *A new agenda for research in educational leadership* (pp. 119–137). New York: Teachers College Press.

Garap, S. (2004). *Kup women for peace: Women taking action to build peace and influence community decision-making.* Canberra, ACT: State Society and Governance in Melanesia Project Research School of Pacific and Asian Studies, Australian National University.

Hall, V. (1993). Women in educational management: A review of research in Britain. In J. Ouston (Ed.), *Women in education management* (pp. 23–46). London: Longman.

Hall, V. (1996). *Dancing on the ceiling: A study of women managers in education*. London: P. Chapman.

Hart, A. W. (1995). Women ascending to leadership: The organizational socialization of principals. In D. M. Dunlap & P. A. Schmuck (Eds.), *Women leading in education* **(pages)**. Albany, NY: SUNY.

Hasibuan-Sedyono, C. (1998). She who manages: The Indonesian woman in management. In P. Drake & P. Owen (Eds.), *Gender and management issues in education: An international perspective* (pp. 83–96). Stoke on Trent, England: Trentham Books.

Hoy, K. W., & Miskel, G. C. (1991). *Educational administration: Theory, research and practice* (4th ed.). New York: McGraw Hill.

Kelep-Malpo, K. D. (2003). *Gender and school leadership in the Papau New Guinea public school system*. Unpublished doctoral thesis, Victoria University of Wellington, Wellington.

Kilavanwa, B. V. L. (2004). *Women leaders in schools in Papua New Guinea: Why do women leaders labor in the shadows?* Unpublished master's thesis, University of Waikato, Hamilton.

Malasa, D. P. (2007). *Effective school leadership: An exploration of issues inhibiting the effectiveness of school leadership in Solomon Islands' secondary schools*. Unpublished master's thesis, University of Waikato, Hamilton.

MEHRD. (2004). *Annual report 2004*. Honiara: Author.

MEHRD. (2005). *Education corporate plan 2006–2008*. Honiara: Author.

MEHRD. (2006). *SIEMIS analysis workbook: Number of qualified and certified teachers in the secondary division* [Table]. Honiara: Author.

MEHRD. (2007). *Solomon Islands teaching service handbook*. Honiara: Author.

Moorosi, P. (2007). Creating linkages between private and public: Challenges facing woman principals in South Africa. *South African Journal of Education, 27*(3), 507–521.

Morris, J. (1998). Good education management: Women's experiences. In P. Drake & P. Owen (Eds.), *Gender and management issues in education: An international perspective* (pp. 97–112). Stoke on Trent, England: Trentham Books.

Narokobi, B. (1983). *Life and leadership in Melanesia by Bernard Narokobi*. Port Moresby: University of Papua New Guinea.

Oplatka, I. (2006). Women in educational administration within developing countries. *Journal of Educational Administration, 44*(6), 604–624.

Pheko, B. (2008). Secondary school leadership practice in Botswana: Implications for effective training. *Educational Management Administration & Leadership, 36*(1), 71–84.

Pollard, A. A. (2000). *Givers of wisdom, labourers without gain: Essays on women in the Solomon Islands*. Honiara: Institute of Pacific Studies and University of the South Pacific Centre in Solomon Islands.

Pollard, A. A. (2006). *Gender and leadership in the 'Are 'Are society, the South Sea Evangelical Church and parliamentary leadership*. Unpublished doctoral thesis, Victoria University of Wellington, Wellington.

Puamu, P. (1998). The principalship in Fiji secondary school: A critical post-colonial perspective in leadership in crisis? In L. Ehrich & K. Knight (Eds.), *Restructuring principled practice: Essays on contemporary educational leadership* (pp. 152–166). Brisbane: Port Press.

Robertson, J. M. (1995). *Theories of leadership: Educational leadership: Issues and perspectives* [lecture notes]. University of Waikato, Hamilton.

Robertson, J. M. (1996). *Are we in the right jungle? Professional partners help New Zealand principals refocus on educational leader* [lecture notes]. University of Waikato, Hamilton.

Sanga, K., & Walker, K. D. (2005). *Apem moa Solomon Islands leadership*. Wellington: He Parekereke, Victoria University of Wellington.

Saunders, R. (2005). Youth leadership: Creating meaningful programmes for young women through a process of co-construction. *New Zealand Journal of Educational Leadership, 20*, 15–30.

Schein, E. H. (1985). *Organization culture and leadership*. San Francisco: Jossey-Bass.

Schmuck, P. A., & Schubert, J. (1995). Women principals' views on sex equity: Exploring issues of integration and information. In D. M. Dunlap & P. A. Schmuck (Eds.), *Women leading in education* (pp. 274–287). Albany, NY: State University of New York Press.

Senge, P. (1990). *The fifth discipline: The art and practice of learning organization*. New York: Double Day Currency.

Sergiovanni, T. J. (1992). *Moral leadership: Getting to the heart of school improvement*. San Francisco: Jossey-Bass.

Shakeshaft, C. (1987). *Women in educational administration*. Newbury Park, CA: Sage.

Sigford, J. L. (2006). *The effective school leader's guide to management*. Thousand Oaks, CA: Corwin Press.

Skrla, L., Reyes, P., & Scheurich, J. (2000). Sexism, silence, and solutions: Women superintendents speak up and speak out. *Educational Administration Quarterly, 36*(1), 44–75.

Strachan, J. (2004). Leadership for social justice. [Editorial] *New Zealand Journal of Educational Leadership, 19*, 3–5.

Strachan, J. M. B. (1991). *Empowering women for educational leadership: A feminist action research project*. Unpublished master's thesis, University of Waikato, Hamilton.

Strachan, J. M. B. (1993). Including the personal and the professional: Researching women in educational leadership. *Gender and Education, 5*(1), 71–80.

Strachan, J. M. B. (2002). *A gender analysis of the education sector in Vanuatu.* Port Vila, Vanuatu: Department of Women's Affairs.

Strachan, J. M. B. (2006). *Educational leadership: Issues and perspectives* [lecture notes]. University of Waikato, Hamilton.

Strachan, J. M. B. (2007, July). *Somebody's daughter: Women and educational leadership in New Zealand and Melanesia.* Paper presented at the Women and Educational Leadership conference, Duquesne University, Rome campus, Italy.

Strachan, J., Saunders, R., Jimmy, L., & Lapi, G. (2007). Ni Vanuatu women and educational leadership development. *New Zealand Journal of Educational Leadership, 22*(2), 37–48.

Tuivaga, J. (1988). Fiji. In T. Tongamoa (Ed.), *Pacific women: Roles and status of women in Pacific societies* (pp. 1–21). Suva: Institute of Pacific Studies of the University of the South Pacific.

Vaa, L. R. (2006). *Women: The Pacific potential* [electronic version]. Retrieved 10 March 2008, from http://www.nzfgw.org.nz/Documents/Pacific-Oct06.pdf

Wallace, H. (2000). Gender and the reform process in Vanuatu and Solomon Islands. *Development Bulletin, 51,* 23–25.

Shalom Akao

Shalom was born in Honiara but completed her early schooling in the Malaitan village of Fouia. She later spent time in Fiji where her parents were studying. After attending high school at Selwyn College she spent a year at the School of Education SICHE, then from 2002-4 completed an undergraduate degree in Social Sciences at The University of Waikato. She taught social studies for four years at St John's College then returned to Waikato to study for a masters degree in Educational Leadership from 2006-8. After graduating she returned to Honiara where she is currently working as a Development Programme Coordinator in Education with the New Zealand High Commission. Shalom is married with three children. She takes a keen interest in sports, especially netball, where she mentors young women and encourages them to be active participants.

SECTION THREE

WIDER CURRICULUM ISSUES

CHAPTER 7
Really Useful Knowledge

Susanne Maezama
School of Education, Solomon Islands College of Higher Education

Introduction

Until recently, the outcomes of education in Solomon Islands schools were those developed by missionaries and the English colonial government. Since independence in 1978 the education system has tried to mirror those of developed nations. The experience of political turmoil from 1998 to 2002 has led Solomon Islanders to believe that the country needs to have a strong education that provides "really useful outcomes". Understanding what such really useful outcomes might be from a Solomon Islands' perspective is therefore necessary.

My master's study, completed in 2000, involved an exploration of literature on really useful knowledge as well as interviews with tertiary leaders at the Solomon Islands College of Higher Education (SICHE). Since then, as Head of the School of Education at SICHE, I have been involved in a partnership programme with the School of Education at the University of Waikato, funded by New Zealand's International Aid and Development Agency (NZAID). The focus of this partnership was on developing capacity in the school and introducing new teacher education programmes. As a result, I was forced to reflect deeply on the content and delivery of our existing programmes and the best way to change them to meet the current needs of schools and students. At the same time the Curriculum Development Centre was working on new curriculum materials for use in schools—resources that would be more relevant to Solomon Islands children in their communities.

This chapter explores the concept of what is really useful knowledge for teachers preparing to work in Solomon Islands schools, and for students. It argues that this knowledge needs to be based on international research on teaching and learning on the one hand, but also on dialogue with the community, the Government and industry on the other hand; and that such knowledge can never be fixed and static, but must change to meet the ongoing challenges faced by our society. I discuss such really useful knowledge using a framework derived from research in developing countries but with local context, and contend that really useful knowledge for the Solomon Islands should produce outcomes such as increased political and critical awareness, the creation of a skilled and competent workforce and improved health.

Educational aims and outcomes in developing countries

Although aspirations for increasing access to education have been positive, the rapid development of education in developing countries across the world has brought problems that continue to be complex and varied in nature (Graham-Brown, 1991; Simmons 1980). Despite expansion, inequalities between developed and developing countries have persisted. Nor has the expansion of education succeeded in eliminating disparities within developing countries, or that between men and women. Some writers suggest that more education has merely created an "indigenous educated elite" (Demerath, 1999,

p. 164) and a growing number of unemployed school leavers. In the Solomon Islands, these problems contributed to the development of community high schools (CHS), which were intended to widen participation in general, allow more girls to attend senior schools and lower costs (Sikua, 2002). At the same time, there was concern that the curriculum should address the real educational needs of village children and equip them to survive in the modern world—not merely provide academic knowledge.

A number of writers have tried to define ideal outcomes for education. These outcomes include human resource development, participation, social justice and the development of strategies for survival. In general, the literature presents ideal outcomes as a means to enhance national development:

> Governments in developing countries gave high priority to education in allocating their resources, reflecting both a strong political will to generalise access to education, in the conviction that it would help foster national unity and satisfy social justice and respect for an essential human right. (Hallak, 1990, p. 7)

In the Solomon Islands, the Curriculum Reform of Secondary Education Policy states that "the endorsed curriculum must show regard for the emerging demands for knowledge and skill for Solomon Islands' culture (MEHRD, 1992, p. 50).

However, much of the literature on educational outcomes stresses economic factors. Titmus (1989) contends that education is preparation for working life. Kaye (1985) comments that governments and employers expect to have their skilled paid workforce needs met through education. Others suggest that education can help increase agricultural and industrial production to enable a country to compete better in local and international markets (Bock & Bock, 1989). Education is also seen as crucial for actively contributing to technological innovation. Those who graduate from Solomon Islands secondary schools, however, frequently find they have no further access to training, or that there is no employment available. Sikua (2002) notes that many community members and officials want the graduates to have the capability to be self-employed as well as working in traditional areas.

For a Solomon Islander reflecting on the ideal aims of education, these commonly espoused views raise problems. In general the literature focuses on Western models, even though the conditions of education and life found in developing countries differ greatly from those in the developed West (Fuller, 1994). This Western model can perpetuate societal inequalities and impart values, attitudes and aspirations not conducive to development in developing countries (Thirlwall, 1999). There is also a growing problem of unemployment among the educated, and students' hopes to escape from poverty through education are often unfulfilled, particularly among the least privileged social groups (Graham-Brown, 1991). Those of us in developing countries need to seriously question some basic assumptions about educational practice. For one thing, it is important to distinguish between formal, nonformal and informal contexts of education rather than seeing education as homogeneous, and to develop theories to underpin the new developments.

The Solomon Islands' context: Theorising about really useful knowledge

Ten years after my initial research was conducted, the Solomon Islands still has a low national literacy rate, but some progress has been made. The number of students staying at school for at least some secondary education has increased dramatically, and there are new curriculum developments that try to make education more relevant to the Solomon Islands' context—and more practical. It is therefore a suitable time to look again at the concept of really useful education.

One useful model for analysing educational needs in the Solomon Islands is Richard Johnson's framework of really useful knowledge (1988). Although he is from the developed world, his work has strengths relevant to our Solomon Islands' context. First, he emphasises that particular knowledges are required in particular contexts; this is congruent with my concern that our context is unique. Second, his critique of upper-class oppression of the working class parallels my concern about first-world colonisers imposing their educational models on developing countries. As will be discussed later in the chapter, his ideas have been applied in practical situations. Because much of the external education in the Solomon Islands is outcomes driven, we need to argue for educational outcomes that are appropriate for our country.

My reading of the literature revealed two major purposes for teaching "really useful knowledge": freedom and practical skills. Knowledge for freedom means knowledge calculated to make people free, and includes the belief in natural rights to secure a government that represents and protects its citizens. It is also knowledge that attempts to explain and/or change the exploitation people can experience in capitalism and knowledge that is legitimate for its users. On the other hand, really useful practical knowledge means the use of skills and ideas for everyday living and survival. It is knowledge that will enable people to enjoy a good life, become good citizens and utilise their leisure time. It also means knowledge of how to do as many things as possible, and knowledge that makes really profound changes in human life.

To construct really useful knowledge outcomes for the Solomon Islands, it is necessary to theorise about them. The process of theorising is a complex one, which requires merging conceptual areas intellectually. It is a kind of "conceptual Mathematics" (J. Stalker, personal communication, 2000), which merges the elements of society, organisation and individual ideal outcomes with knowledge for freedom and practical knowledge. If we undertake this "conceptual mathematic", we enrich the ideas on the ideal outcomes of education in developing countries with the ideas of outcomes associated with really useful knowledge.

The really useful educational outcomes expected in developing countries such as the Solomon Islands can be classified under three major categories: increased political and critical awareness; the creation of a skilled and competent workforce; and improved health.

Increased critical and political awareness

Increasing critical and political awareness may result in students developing responsible attitudes and behaviour, both in the workplace and more generally in society. In addition, they can be expected to develop skills, knowledge and attitudes to participate in activities that promote both economic growth and a positive response to social change. One aspect of this is respect for other people's points of view and public and private property. Consideration of citizens' rights also means recognising and supporting their need for access to formal education. Another important outcome expected is the ability to critique development projects. Their education should equip students with the skills and knowledge to assess such projects, at both the national and community levels, in terms of their appropriateness to the situations in which they are implemented.

Two further outcomes in this category are familiarity with the society's history and culture and a capacity for leadership. A desirable outcome of education would be the development of a deep understanding of existing political, economic, educational and social structures to underpin students' ability to be critical of issues that affect their societies, communities and families. A consequence of this ability and knowledge is the development of leadership capacity, and the ability to make sound decisions in the paid workforce and in their communities.

The creation of a skilled and competent paid workforce

We might expect to find two outcomes in this category. The first is the expectation that education will increase innovators' and entrepreneurs' ability to create employment in the form of new businesses or industries. At the same time, these innovators are creating new businesses to absorb school leavers. Education is expected to encourage students to look for other ways of earning a living than relying on the Government to provide employment. Education can instil in students the knowledge of the variety of employment choices available to them.

A second really useful educational outcome is the expectation that students will be trained with the necessary skills, attitudes and behaviour that will enable them to be employable in both the private and public sectors. It is also expected to provide leaders capable of taking up responsibility as supervisors or managers in industries.

Improved health

Under this category we might expect to find a really useful educational outcome that involves the practice of a healthy social lifestyle. Education should contribute to the ways individuals and communities practise healthy social lifestyles by exposing them to social habits that are both beneficial and detrimental to the livelihoods of people and of the nation. For example, they could learn about the importance of hygiene in food preparation, problems caused by nonbiodegradable rubbish such as plastic, the dangers of unprotected sex and the importance of exercise for those in more sedentary lifestyles. People will thus make informed decisions at home, at work and in their communities. The improvement of basic health and hygiene at the personal, community and national levels depends on access to, and maintenance of, water supplies and sanitation facilities.

Investigating educators' views

Ten years ago I completed my research interviewing tertiary educators in the Solomon Islands to see how their ideas about really useful knowledge fitted with my theorising. At that time the country was in turmoil because of the ethnic tensions, but these tertiary leaders had an ambitious agenda. They were most concerned that education should help students understand their own country, history and culture. They believed this would help to achieve peace and harmony in our society. They also felt that students should learn to be critical and aware of the political processes of the country. They saw an important outcome of education as the development of responsible attitudes and behaviour through the inculcation of values. Whereas traditional values emphasised loyalty to family, village and tribal groups, these educators had a vision that widened loyalty to and responsibility for the nation as well as local loyalties.

My interviewees also believed that education should develop skilled and competent people for the paid workforce, who are able to meet the needs of industry as senior employees in Solomon Islands organisations and industries. This included developing personal skills in relating to others, and leadership skills. Going further, they suggested that creating employment would be a really useful educational outcome. This could happen if students' education helped them to become innovators and entrepreneurs, able to start businesses themselves and to become self-employed in areas such as running small workshops for small engineering repairs, carpentry, surveying, plumbing or electrical fittings, or owning their own retail stores, fish markets and so on.

The respondents also saw improved health as a really useful outcome of education. Healthy social lifestyles for individuals are a means to improve both the individual's and the community's health. This includes developing acceptable ways to interact with others in the community, which is a step towards living in peace and harmony.

Improved healthy social lifestyles for the individual can also improve the community's social habits, such as the misuse of alcohol, and sexually transmitted diseases. People need to understand the impact of these habits on individuals, their jobs and their communities.

An interesting finding was that the respondents tended to see really useful educational outcomes as homogeneous and did not overtly acknowledge the impact of diversity. Yet factors such as gender, age, ability and sexuality must be considered. Not everyone has the same problems, and so the same solutions do not work for everyone. They did, however, see that really useful educational outcomes need to be at three levels: societal, organisational and individual.

In summary, the respondents' beliefs were congruent with the theorising I undertook. Nevertheless, I noted that their responses were much influenced by their context and were often bounded by the unit in which they worked. It was hard for them to take an institutional-wide view, and much more difficult again to envisage a national perspective. They also placed considerable emphasis on individual development (not surprisingly, as they taught individuals) rather than social development, which they may have seen as outside their influence. But they did want their students to develop a political awareness and be able to critique such issues as development projects funded by external donors. Society would benefit most if aid projects had considerable local input and did not have the direction of development dictated externally.

Some problematic issues were raised in the responses. First, it seemed as though the problem of unemployment was being placed on the individual to solve. While many people may have established their own businesses, it is doubtful that this can be used as the main strategy to solve the Solomon Islands' unemployment problems. Second, although it is laudable to try to equip students with responsible attitudes and behaviours, this may also place undue burdens on the individual. Third, the emphasis on individuals fostering change may be at variance with traditional cultural values that privilege collectivism and collective responsibility. Likewise, it is problematic to rely on individuals adopting healthy lifestyles as a means to improve the community's health. Often community health depends on the improvement of basic amenities that sustain life. People in rural areas often do not have access to proper sanitation and water supplies. Individuals may not be able to change this, and expecting them to do so is simply an example of "blaming the victim". The Government needs to act to ensure these essentials are provided.

Changes in Solomon Islands education since 2004

By 2004 the country was returning to normal and trying to establish harmony after the end of the ethnic tensions. According to Sade (2009), many people held Solomon Islands education responsible for some of the underlying tensions, since the curriculum was largely academic rather than technical and was seen as contributing to unemployment. Sikua (2002) had found that many communities that established CHS had similar concerns about the curriculum and thought it was not helping students gain skills for self-employment or village life. In addition, it was felt that such education was often alienating young people from their own culture and language. It could be argued, therefore, that it was not producing really useful educational outcomes.

Changes implemented by the Ministry of Education and Human Resources Development (MEHRD) since 2004, with the support of various external aid agencies, have focused on increasing access to education, developing a new contextually relevant curriculum and resources and enhancing quality in teaching and greater co-operation and co-ordination between sectors. The MEHRD's reforms are in line with the key elements of really useful educational outcomes discussed earlier in this chapter: education for practical living and education for freedom.

Curriculum Development Centre

The Education Sector Investment Reform Programme (2004) has guided the current National Curriculum Statement (2008) in developing a new contextually relevant curriculum and resources for early childhood education, primary and secondary schools, and technical vocational education and training (TVET). The reform emphasises education for life, through which the relevant knowledge, skills and attitudes can be acquired. It stresses that the learning opportunities offered should enable learners to live in harmony with others and with their environment, and prepare them for adult life and making a living.

Furthermore, the national curriculum is promoting a shift from a curriculum defined in terms of subject content, to a curriculum defined in terms of what learners are expected to understand, know, be able to do and be able to appreciate. This approach is concerned with the achievement of learning outcomes. It is learner focused and outcomes driven. This means the syllabuses do not focus on the content of the subject, but on how learners may be able to make use of that content to benefit their own lives. The curriculum also acknowledges that learning is a process by which individuals gain fundamental knowledge, skills, competencies, attitudes, values, beliefs and symbolic systems to enable them to live productive personal lives and to live successfully with their family, their community, the wider Solomon Islands society and the world beyond.

Technology curriculum

Following criticism that education focused too strongly on academic rather than practical skills, the MEHRD developed a new policy for technical and vocational training in 2004. This was followed by major curriculum reform for technology in 2005/06 and a series of intensive professional development workshops for teachers in 2006. The changes that were made reflected international thinking on technological education and aimed to develop both understanding and technological literacy (see also Chapter 7). The new curriculum aimed to bridge the gap between creativity and technical skills, and to encourage students to design solutions to technical problems. Technology was to be understood as "processes used for solving technical problems to meet the needs of society", based on "teachers' designing problem solving based activities" (Sade, 2009, p. 186). The curriculum was also intended to develop students' awareness of the social impact of technology. These far-reaching changes to the technology curriculum thus aimed to increase the critical awareness of students, and to develop useful practical skills.

Teacher education partnership

An NZAID-sponsored partnership between the University of Waikato and the Solomon Islands School of Education at SICHE from 2006 to 2010 embarked on the review, revision and upgrading of the teacher education programmes, courses and organisational processes at the Solomon Islands School of Education. This has resulted in the implementation of four new teacher education qualifications at the School of Education in 2009. Both the structure of the qualifications and the content of the courses have been radically changed, improved and updated. The teacher education programme offered is unique, in that it specifically focuses on preparing teachers for the Solomon Islands. It encourages student teachers to become independent, critical, creative and caring lifelong learners and practitioners. This means that the quality of teacher education at the School of Education has been significantly raised and is now comparable with best practice teacher education elsewhere.

Untrained teachers

A major activity undertaken to improve the quality of teachers was the design and delivery of the Certificate in Teaching for Primary and Secondary Teachers for teachers in training. This programme was developed by the School of Education in partnership with the University of Waikato. It consisted of four six-week courses involving lectures, tutorials, assignments and individual mentoring, delivered at the School of Education campus in Honiara from June 2007 to February 2009. It was reported that the training the teachers in training received contributed to their practice in the classroom. Thompson (2010) reported that:

> the motivation that teachers had in wanting to use more student centred activities and try out group work showed that the courses had impacted on their views of effective teaching and learning activities. (p. 12)

The report further reiterated that the graduates had a real sense of achievement and gained more confidence in their abilities to study and apply new approaches to learning and teaching.

Emphasis on quality

The MEHRD has developed a *National Education Action Plan 2010–2012*. Goal 2 in this plan emphasises quality of education in the Solomon Islands. The plan aims to achieve an outcome whereby all levels and dimensions of the Solomon Islands consistently demonstrate standards of excellence and deliver a quality education. This means a high quality of learning achieved through the provision of an adequate number of qualified teachers and other workers in the education sector, a relevant national school curriculum and local curricula, an adequate number of modern, relevant teaching and learning materials or facilities and sound standards of student literacy and numeracy.

Continued growth and support for CHS: Access, community ownership and curriculum

A major evaluation of the rapid development of CHS (Sikua, 2002) found that communities around the country were hungry for greater access to education and were willing to work with the Government and the MEHRD to help fund school buildings and facilities (see also Chapter 1). The continued growth of the CHS system has made it possible for a far greater numbers of students—both male and female—to attend secondary school and to do so close to home so that strong links between family, school and community can be forged and maintained. The sense of ownership of and support for these local schools is strong, and parents no longer feel that their children will lose touch with their roots by attending boarding schools far from home.

However, the evaluation also found that the academic curriculum still in place in the 1990s was not always suited to the needs of the students and did not necessarily prepare them for life in the villages or for self-employment. The extremely rapid expansion also meant that resources were stretched very thinly or were lacking, and that teachers were not always qualified to teach across the curriculum. Since then there have been significant changes to the curriculum, with the development of new classroom materials designed specifically for the Solomon Islands' context. The developments endorsed by the Solomon Islands Government and its Ministry of Education (MEHRD) are thus geared to encouraging secondary schooling that develops practical skills and ensures that knowledge is related to the local context.

Co-ordination between education sectors

The Government's development of the Sector Wide Approach (SWAp), whereby all levels of education and many participants are involved, should facilitate the development of broader, more integrated and practical curriculum. The development, implementation, monitoring and revision of selected strategies and their related activities are based on carrying out consultative processes with all stakeholders, such as national and provincial governments, education staff at all levels, students, children and communities, development partners and nongovernment organisations.

This sector dialogue is managed by a co-ordination team and a management team, and supported by technical working groups, an education sector co-ordination committee, an education sector governance committee and through the mechanisms of an annual joint review, a performance assessment framework and the Solomon Islands Education and Management Information System.

Conclusion

As we have seen, really useful knowledge is a complex concept. When I completed my master's thesis I was able to confirm my ideas through a variety of research. Those I interviewed were clear that increased political and critical awareness and the creation of a skilled and competent workforce are important. They believed that meeting the needs of industries and the creation of employment through innovators and entrepreneurs are important educational outcomes for the Solomon Islands. My ideas concerning the value of improved health through social and physical lifestyles were also confirmed. Thus the use of Johnson's theory proved to be appropriate to create a framework applicable to the Solomon Islands' setting.

My research in 2000 also highlighted some absences in the literature on really useful educational outcomes. The participants in my study identified really useful educational outcomes that were not evident in the literature, such as the creation of responsible attitudes and behaviour, the enhancement of positive change, the creation of employment through innovators and entrepreneurs, the development of good leadership and the practice of healthy social lifestyles. These areas remain crucial in Pacific Island nations.

In this chapter I have focused on policy changes made by the MEHRD, especially in the development of new curricula for schools and the establishment of CHS; changes that have taken place within the School of Education at SICHE; and efforts to enhance quality across the education system and promote collaboration. I have found that these initiatives have aimed to increase student engagement in critical thinking related to their own context, and to provide the opportunities to gain practical skills. This is in line with claims in the literature that a relevant education is one that enables people to have the skills to deal competently with everyday life, in order to create a strong society (Avalos, 1992; Bock & Bock, 1989).

The School of Education at SICHE now aims to produce teachers who are independent, critical, creative and caring lifelong learners and practitioners. The MEHRD's policy framework tries to ensure that sectors work together to meet the aim of providing access to quality education for all. Although the problem of youth unemployment remains, there has been a serious attempt to provide school leavers with really useful education, which incorporates their local knowledge as well as more internationally developed knowledge. Much more could be done, such as community education through CHS, but MEHRD's three aims—access, practicality and quality—are significant pointers to really useful educational outcomes for our country. We must not lose sight of education for freedom and for practical living.

References

Avalos, B. (1992) Education for the poor: Quality or relevance. *British Journal of Education, 1*(4), 419–436.

Bock, J., & Bock, C. (1989). Non-formal education policy: Developing countries. In C. Titmus (Ed.), *Lifelong education for adults: An international handbook* (pp. 64–69). Oxford: Pergamon Press.

Demerath, P. (1999). The cultural production of educational utility in Pere village, Papua New Guinea. *Comparative Education Review, 43*(2), 162–192.

Fuller, B. (1994). Quality of education in developing nations: Policies for improving. In T. Husen & T. Postlethwaite (Eds.), *The international encyclopaedia of education, Volume 8* (pp. 4865–4873). New York: Pergamon Press.

Graham-Brown, S. (1991). *Education in the developing countries: Conflict and crises.* London: Longman.

Hallak, J. (1990). *Investing in the future: Setting priorities in the developing world.* Oxford: Pergamon Press.

Johnson, R. (1988). "Really useful knowledge": Radical education and working class culture, 1790–1850: Memories for education in the 1980s. In T. Lovett (Ed.), *Radical approaches to adult education: A reader* (pp. 3–34). London: Routledge.

Kaye, T. (1985). What kind of graduates should USP produce? *Pacific Perspectives, 12*(1), 29–38.

MEHRD. (1992). *Solomon Islands third education and training project*. Honiara: Author.

Sade, D. (2009). *Professional development for a new curriculum in a developing country: The example of technology education in the Solomon Islands*. Unpublished doctoral thesis, University of Waikato, Hamilton.

Sikua, D. (2002). *Decentralisation and community high schools in the Solomon Islands*. Unpublished doctoral thesis, University of Waikato, Hamilton.

Simmons, J. (1980). *The education dilemma: Policy issues for developing countries in the 1980s*. Oxford: Pergamon Press.

Thirlwall, A. (1999). *Growth and development*. London: Macmillan.

Thompson, P. (2010). *Solomon Islands evaluation of the School of Education's Certificate in Teaching for Teachers in Training Program (TIT)*. Honiara: MEHRD.

Titmus, C. (1989). Adult education for employment: Purpose and principles. In C. Titmus (Ed.), *Lifelong education for adults: An international handbook* (pp. 93–95). Oxford: Pergamon.

Susanne Maezama

Susanne was born on Isabel where she received her primary education at boarding school from years 3-7. Her secondary education took place at Selwyn College in Guadalcanal after which she attended Goroka Teachers College, where she gained a Diploma in Teaching Secondary. Then she attended the South Australian College of Advanced Education where she gained her Bachelor of Teaching majoring in textile studies. She taught in a rural National Secondary School in Makira before moving to the School of Education SICHE as a lecturer in home economics and education. She completed a masters degree at the University of Waikato in 2000 and on her return to the Solomons taught in a rural secondary school on Isabel. She returned to the School of Education in 2004 as Head of Science and served as Head of School from 2007-2010. Susanne is married with three children and maintains interests in gardening, reading, designing and making clothing and household goods.

CHAPTER 8
The Impact of Effective Professional Development on Technical Education in the Solomon Islands

David Sade
Solomon Islands College of Higher Education

Introduction

For the first three years of the 21st century the Solomon Islands underwent a period of civil unrest. Many of those seeking the root of the ethnic tension that caused this unrest came to believe that the policies of the Ministry of Education and Human Resources Development (MEHRD) were partly to blame (MEHRD, 2004a). They claimed that education policies and practices were heavily biased towards academic rather than technical education, and that the rise in unemployment was partly the result of students lacking practical skills. In response, the national government, through the MEHRD, established a task force to revisit its policies and practices with the aim of striking a balance between academic and technical education. Consequently, a Technical and Vocational Education Training (TVET) policy was developed to provide that balance (MEHRD, 2004a). This resulted in a major curriculum reform undertaken by the MEHRD in 2004 and 2005. Technology education was one of the subjects to undergo changes as an outcome of the education reforms.

In 2005 I was asked to leave my teaching position at Betikama High School to carry out a project for the Curriculum Development Centre to research and develop a professional development programme for technology education that took into account the local context, teachers' views and best practices that focused on enhancing teacher knowledge to influence curriculum implementation. The preliminary findings in 2005 set the basis for the professional development intervention programme undertaken in 2006. It was based on key professional development principles of teacher support and teacher reflection and sharing, and it was ongoing. As the professional development provider employed to help bring about teacher change, I used a social constructivist learning model. The programme built on localised context and was crafted around best practices from other professional development models. However, contributing to the difficulties of curriculum reform in the Solomon Islands are its developing nature, the backdrop of civil unrest and the geographic spread of its many islands.

This chapter explores issues encountered in the development and delivery of this professional development programme. In one sense it is therefore an examination of my own practice. Obviously I have a personal interest in evaluating the success of the new curriculum, teachers' understanding of it and the effectiveness of the workshop programme as a whole, but the requirements of the doctoral programme ensured the study was rigorous in conception and implementation. This chapter provides a valuable record of an important innovation, demonstrates the efficacy of the professional development model used and concludes that it could well be adopted in other areas.

Context

Technology education is a new development for teachers in the Solomon Islands. Recent changes made to the existing industrial arts curriculum reflect much of the technology education curriculum reform that has occurred in other countries. The aim of the new curriculum is to develop technological literacy through an ongoing learning process and solve problems through the design process approach. The design process engages students in identifying problems, needs or opportunities in real-life situations within the Solomon Islands' context. This is a new approach compared to the more prescribed technical education that teachers are used to.

The ultimate aim of the new technology curriculum is to educate students to become knowledgeable and technically skilful, and to be aware of the social impacts and effects of technology and society, both within the Solomon Islands' context and globally (MEHRD, 2005). The curriculum reform reflects a broader technological literacy approach comprising technological knowledge, technological process and technological and societal values. Thus, the development of teachers' knowledge of technology and technology education, and their technology education practices, are crucial for the successful implementation of the new curriculum.

Professional development (PD) workshops are restricted to school mid-year holidays and are always held centrally at Honiara. The geographical spread of islands in the Solomon Islands is the key factor influencing the infrequency of the PD workshops. Although PD is seen as important, it does not receive ongoing support due to the scattered population, the isolation of many schools and the difficulties of travel. Because of the challenges faced by the education system in the Solomon Islands there is enormous potential for PD, and there is ample evidence that teachers are eager to participate in PD programmes.

The purpose of the study on which this chapter is based was to develop, implement and evaluate a PD model to be used for preparing technology teachers for the implementation of the new technology curriculum in the Solomon Islands. The study took into account the teachers' existing perceptions of technology and technology education, classroom practices and student learning. The effect of the PD intervention was explored, investigated and evaluated by re-examining the teachers' views, classroom practices and student learning following the intervention. Data generation for this study was guided by the following research questions:

1. What are the teachers' existing views of technology and technology education, and their current classroom practices?
2. What is an appropriate professional development model for technology education in the Solomon Islands?
3. What effect and influence does a professional development programme have on teachers' concepts of technology and technology education, and their classroom practices?
4. What is the impact of teachers' developing understandings and practices in technology education on student learning?

Methods

The theoretical framework for the study was grounded within the interpretivist paradigm, using a qualitative case study approach. This study was undertaken with eight secondary technology education teachers in Honiara over a period of two years in 2005 and 2006. The preliminary inquiry of this study was undertaken in 2005, with a follow-up intervention study in 2006. Semistructured interviews were used as the key method for data gathering in both phases. The teachers' existing perceptions in 2005 and their change of perceptions after the PD intervention in 2006 were generated through the semistructured interview approach.

Other methods used for data generation in this study were classroom observation and documents from teachers' and students' work. Participant observation was adopted for gathering data on classroom practices in 2005 and 2006, and also during the PD intervention in 2006. Documents containing teachers' teaching lessons and students' work were analysed for triangulation purposes.

Findings

The preliminary inquiry

The preliminary inquiry in 2005 showed that technology teachers in the Solomon Islands held narrow perspectives of technology and technology education, with views centring on the purely technical aspects. The views teachers held on technology, indigenous technology, technology education and the worth of technology education were varied, and included technology as artefacts, technology as making something and technology as the application of knowledge. Teachers viewed indigenous technology as being to do with traditional practices in the Solomon Islands, and technology education as technically oriented education. Viewing technology education through this technical lens meant that it was perceived by these teachers as suitable for the less academic students, and particularly useful for making a living in rural communities. As these teachers had a technical education teaching background, the influences of subject subculture and background experiences were evident (Jones & Carr, 1992). Overall, the findings showed that teachers' knowledge of the nature of technology and technology education was narrow and limited.

The teachers' 2005 classroom practices were very conservative, with technical skills-focused teaching approaches using mainly rote learning, and their assessment was dominated by summative assessment. Teachers' views of technology education as technically oriented education strongly influenced their views of classroom activities and teaching strategies. Teachers associated their existing technical classroom practices with technological pedagogy in technology education. These practices included textbook-based procedural knowledge for practical activities, and the skilful use of tools when undertaking practical tasks. The teachers' teaching documents were mainly based on the prescribed MEHRD textbooks or teacher-prepared teaching documents. Both types of teaching documents were predominantly prescriptive, with teachers using them as recipe books on which their teaching lessons were based.

Few of the teachers' learning outcomes were written down because most of the teaching documents were based on the MEHRD textbooks, which do not outline clear learning outcomes. As a result, the teachers' learning outcomes were verbally expressed and based on the content of the prescribed document. Most of the teachers' documentation contained notes emphasising either a process involved in manufacturing a product, or working procedures involved in acquiring a technical skill. The teaching of particular procedures was also emphasised in most of the teaching lessons. Both teaching documents and practices emphasised particular working procedures.

All the teachers taught their theoretical lessons separately from their practical lessons. This practice was influenced by two factors. First, the school's organisation meant that teachers had no choice but to organise their teaching lessons to fit in with the school timetables. Second, the lack of administrative support, and the lack of facilities and equipment experienced by the teachers from various schools, caused difficulties in teaching the theoretical knowledge and practical hands-on activities together. As mentioned, most teachers' teaching approaches focused on a narrow technical approach to technology. This meant that when they did teach practical lessons for hands-on experience they kept to closed tasks that were confined to the outlined prescriptions in the handbook. About half of the teacher participants based their teaching lessons on Curriculum Development Centre-produced textbooks. As a result, most classroom tasks undertaken by students were prescribed tasks, and taken directly from these textbooks.

Because the students' learning was very structured and they were directed to work from the textbook contents exactly as prescribed, on completion all the students' projects looked very much alike as all students did almost the same thing. The students' theoretical lessons were also prescribed in a step-by-step approach. The teachers' teaching approaches were mostly teacher centred, so that students did not have much input on how a task should be done. Students followed the teachers' instructions precisely, as required. These instructions were used as the only student guide to follow for the given tasks. The classrooms were used as the only site for teaching and learning. None of the lessons had links with any community enterprises, or exposed students to any technological community practices, despite the accessibility of numerous enterprises surrounding the schools.

The teachers' view of assessment focused on assessment of learning. The curriculum assessment policy had a strong influence on the teachers' assessment practices. The difference between summative and formative assessment, and how they could be used in assessing student learning, was not clearly understood by the teachers, who had a narrow understanding of formative assessment. Their interactions were one-sided on the teachers' part, with students rarely responding to the teachers' questions. The students' responses were very limited, as most of the teachers' questions were closed, such that there was only one right answer. Formative interactions in the classroom did not pursue students' ideas.

The teachers used both informal and formal kinds of summative assessment. The informal summative assessment involved the teachers spot checking the students' understanding of the lessons being taught. For this the teachers used recall questions, checking on students' understanding of the given tasks, assuming that students would ask questions when they did not understand something, and covering the content within the given time. More formal forms of summative assessment were limited to two approaches: assessing students' completed tasks and giving students a written test. Theoretical lessons were assessed using a written test, and the outcomes of the practical tasks were assessed after the completion of the task.

The findings confirmed that teachers' actual classroom practices were also technical education oriented, matching the views they held on technology and technology education. Enhancing these teachers' understanding of the nature of technology and technology education, and their understanding of technology teaching pedagogy, has the potential to influence their classroom practices in and teach the technology curriculum as intended. Thus it could be argued that a proper understanding of the nature of technology and technology education, of appropriate teaching pedagogy and of assessment practices for learning is imperative if teachers are to teach the technology curriculum in the Solomon Islands effectively.

The intervention programme

The PD intervention programme undertaken by teacher participants during the second phase of the research study was used to help teachers develop a better understanding of the nature of technology and technology education, and basically to help improve their classroom practices in teaching the technology curriculum as intended. The key principles considered effective for PD programmes elsewhere were adopted. These principles were ongoing PD, the learning through reflection approach and teacher support (Bell, 2005; Bell & Gilbert, 1996; Jones, 2003; Jones & Moreland, 2004), including the sharing of classroom experiences.

The incorporation of these strategies aimed to enhance the teachers' existing concepts of technology and technology education and their teaching approaches. The finding was that it was seen to be of great benefit by the teacher participants. The ongoing nature of the PD programme, with the workshop days followed by classroom practice sessions, motivated the teacher participants to implement the concepts and practices learnt from the earlier workshops, and encouraged them to share their classroom experiences with colleagues in the later workshops. The teacher support approach enabled teachers to build confidence in implementing the new concepts in the classroom setting. The teachers indicated that the time spent sharing experiences with others during the workshops was a learning experience. The content delivered in the three workshops contributed positively to teacher change, both in their perceptions of technology and technology education and in their classroom practices in technology education.

The nature of this PD programme was appreciated by teachers because it was very different from their previous PD programmes. The change in their perceptions was achieved through a better understanding of the nature of technology and technology education. Teachers were also keen to undertake changes to their previous teaching practices as a result of the focus of the PD programme on best practice and the use of appropriate pedagogies in teaching technology education. The positive outcome experienced by these teachers during their teaching practice empowered them to embrace the new changes.

The 2006 findings revealed that teachers' previously held perceptions of technology and technology education had changed. The teachers' views of technology changed from technology as artefacts, and as making something and applying technical knowledge, to technology as a process used for solving technological problems to meet the needs of society. Technology education as hands-on activity, technical education and creative activity changed to technology education as design problem-solving-based activities.

The teachers' changed views of technology and technology education showed that they had moved away from their limited range of views of technology and technology education.

The PD programme had a measureable impact on teachers' classroom practices in 2006. The findings showed that every teacher attempted to change some aspects of their classroom practices, including:
- teachers writing lesson plans with clear learning outcomes
- teachers teaching without using the prescribed MEHRD documents (syllabus and textbooks)
- teachers integrating theoretical lessons with their practical lessons
- teachers following an open-ended, problem-solving approach.

The teachers' changed teaching approaches included:
- the use of a context-based teaching approach
- consideration of community involvement in student tasks
- the use of a design process teaching approach.

The teachers' assessment practices also changed, as teacher–student formative assessments became more like reciprocal conversations. Summative assessment also broadened to include a wider range of assessment criteria for student assessment.

The effects of the changed teaching practices on teacher decision making included their trying out the changed teaching practices with additional classes as well as the observed classes, and their decision to continue with their enhanced teaching practices in the years following the research. The factors that hindered teachers were the need for a uniform product to be mass produced; time limits; lack of materials, equipment and tools; and school-based assessment and external examination requirements.

Teachers' enhanced understanding of the nature of technology and technology education, and their changed classroom practices, had a flow-on impact on student learning. Unlike the students' learning experiences in 2005, which were mainly based on technical hands-on learning, the 2006 students' learning experiences were much broader, and included students becoming active learners. The students commented positively on the changes. They preferred the learning approaches that transformed their learning from traditional passive learning in 2005, based on textbook contents and technical hands-on focused activities. In contrast, their 2006 learning changed to active learning and included a range of activities based on the design process approach.

The extent to which the students experienced changes to their learning in 2006 varied between teachers, and depended on the extent of changes the individual teachers were willing to undertake in their teaching practices. The teachers who undertook more changes in their teaching practices in 2006 also provided their students with more learning experiences when carrying out their technology tasks.

Discussion

This study provided empirical evidence that the PD intervention programme had a positive impact on the teachers' perceptions of technology and technology education, and on teachers' teaching practices, which changed from having a technical education focus to a technology education focus. There were strong links between teachers' perceptions and their classroom practices. When teachers developed robust knowledge about technology and technology education, and used appropriate technology education-specific pedagogies, they were able to successfully implement the new Solomon Islands technology education curriculum. The positive impact of the PD programme on teachers' understanding of the nature of technology and technology education, their classroom practices and student learning demonstrate its effectiveness.

The success of the PD model justifies recommending its wider use in other developing countries with similar contexts and situations to the Solomon Islands.

In 2005 the teachers' range of views on technology and indigenous technology mainly reflected artefact-related perspectives. Their view of technology education reflected technical education concepts. These views were narrow perspectives of technology and technology education. The artefacts imported into the Solomon Islands were a major factor influencing teachers' views of technology. The transition from traditional materials into the modern era was the main factor influencing teachers' views of indigenous technology, and the teachers' technical education background was the main factor influencing the teachers' views of technology education. Technology education was viewed by most teachers as a crucial subject, particularly suitable for less academic students. Teachers' traditional classroom practices were conservative and dominated by the teachers. Strict use of the prescribed textbook was the main teaching approach, and it focused on the use of hand tools for skills development. Students' tasks were mainly closed, and focused largely on following working procedures. The teachers' assessment practices indicated that they had limited understanding of either assessments for learning or summative assessment.

The impact of the three key principles (ongoing workshops, teacher reflections and sharing and teacher support) underpinning the PD programme was effective for enhancing and building teachers' confidence to undertake changes. Teachers' views of technology changed from artefact-related perspectives to a process used for solving problems and meeting needs in society. Teachers' views of technology education changed from a technical education perspective to design activities with a problem-solving focus. The teachers' changes in teaching practices included planning more comprehensive and specific technology lessons, teaching open tasks, using a design process, encouraging student self-assessment and covering a broader range of criteria in summative assessment.

These changes all had an impact on student learning. Students changed to active learning, including designing their own technological artefacts, researching information, undertaking self-assessment of their task through reflection exercises, active discussions in group work and constructing their designed artefacts. However, in some cases the issues of uniformity, limited time and examination requirements were an impediment to these changes. Some teachers were motivated to use the new teaching approaches in extra classes, concurrently with the PD programme, and some planned to use them in the future.

Conclusion

A PD intervention programme is crucial for effecting teacher change, and particularly for enhancing teacher knowledge in technology and technology education and their classroom practices (Fox-Turnbull, 2006; Jones & Moreland, 2004). My study showed that the PD invention programme teachers undertook broadened their understanding of technology and technology education and enhanced their classroom practices. The teachers' broadened knowledge of the nature of technology and technology education, along with their enhanced classroom practices, also affected student learning in technology education. The findings indicated that the impact of this PD model was effective for transforming technical education teachers into technology education teachers.

There were strong links between teachers' perceptions and their classroom practices. When teachers developed robust knowledge about technology and technology education, and used appropriate specific technology education pedagogies, they were able to successfully implement the new Solomon Islands technology education curriculum. The positive impact of the PD programme on teachers' understanding of the nature of technology and technology education, their classroom practices and student learning demonstrates its effectiveness. The success of the PD model justifies recommending its wider use in other areas, such as for technology inservice teachers in the Solomon Islands, preservice technology teachers and teacher educators, teachers of other subject areas and technology education teachers in developing countries with similar contexts and situations to the Solomon Islands.

References

Bell, B. (2005). *Learning in science: The Waikato research*. London: Taylor & Francis Group, RoutledgeFalmer.

Bell, B., & Gilbert, J. (1996). *Teacher development: A model from science education*. London: Falmer Press.

Jones, A. (2003). Developing a national curriculum in technology for New Zealand. *International Journal of Technology and Design Education, 13*, 83–99.

Jones, A., & Carr, M. (1992). Teachers' perceptions of technology education: Implications for curriculum innovation. *Research in Science Education, 22*, 230–239.

Jones, A., & Moreland, J. (2004). Enhancing primary teachers' pedagogical content knowledge in technology. *International Journal of Technology and Design Education, 14*, 121–140.

MEHRD. (2004a). *Education for living: Draft policy on technical, vocational education and training*. Honiara: Author.

MEHRD. (2004b). *Education strategic plan 2004–2006* (2nd ed.). Honiara: Author.

MEHRD. (2005). *Technology syllabus: Draft copy*. Honiara: Author.

David Sade

David was born on Malaita where he attended primary school before moving on to board at Betikama Adventist College in Honiara. He gained a Bachelor of Education majoring in Industrial Arts and Agriculture at Pacific Adventist College and taught in Papua New Guinea before returning to Betikama College, first as Head of the Industrial Technology Department. After gaining a postgraduate diploma in Technology Education and a masters degree in Education from The University of Waikato he became Head of the Technology Department at Betikama College. He chaired the Solomon Islands Technology Curriculum panel and was seconded to the Curriculum Development Centre to design and implement professional development for teachers nationally. After the award of his doctorate from the University of Waikato in 2010 he took up the position of Head of the School of Industrial Development at SICHE. David is married. His interests include sport, travel, and spending time in workshops. He is an active member of the Seventh Day Adventist Church.

CHAPTER 9
Technology Teachers' Perceptions of Access to and Use of ICT Tools in Solomon Islands Schools

Solomon Vaji Pita
Lecturer in Technology Education, School of Education
Solomon Islands College of Higher Education

Introduction

My interest in investigating technology teachers' use of and belief in information and communication technology (ICT) in education began when I introduced a basic ICT training module for technology teacher trainees at the School of Education at Solomon Islands College of Higher Education (SICHE), where I was a lecturer from 2004 to 2007. Teacher trainees were excited by their experience and expressed their desire to have an ICT course to learn more. This wish could not easily be achieved because of the lack of ICT development in education in the Solomon Islands, including at the School of Education.

Even so, some schools in the country have acquired photocopy machines and computers, and are connected to the Internet (Leeming, 2003). Having taught for 18 years (10 years as a secondary school technology education teacher and eight years as a lecturer in technology education at the School of Education), I saw that teachers were keen to integrate ICT in their teaching but struggled because of the lack of technical, infrastructural, hardware and professional assistance. I recognised a need to investigate the use of ICT tools in schools, particularly in terms of how teachers integrate them into their teaching practice. I wanted to know how teachers use ICT tools, what challenges they face in doing so and their perceptions of the role of ICT in the Solomon Islands.

Context

Although there is currently no policy to guide the use of ICT in education, schools in the Solomon Islands are beginning to integrate ICT into their teaching. The Solomon Islands Government has undertaken various projects aimed at providing access to education for all its people. Both the *National Education Action Plan 2007–2009* and the previous *Education Action Plan 2004–2006* were government initiatives intended to provide basic education for all (MEHRD, 2004, 2007). These plans allowed for educational innovations such as the use of ICT tools introduced and managed in schools by the People First Network (PFNET), the Distance Learning Centres and the One Laptop Per Child projects. These projects are all hosted in schools where teachers (including technology teachers) become the users, managers and experts to guide students in accessing, using and integrating ICT.

The projects mentioned above have implications for my research because a major aim of all three projects is to provide people with access to education. The relevance of these projects to my study relates to the need to develop ICT infrastructure, provide ICT access to teachers and students, and the development of knowledge and skills among teachers, who are the first group of people trained to use the ICT tools by the three projects. These gaps need to be addressed before ICT can be widely used in schools in this country.

Research design

The data collected for this research project used qualitative research methods to gain insight into the participants' behaviours, value systems, concerns, motivations and aspirations in relation to how they perceive the integration of ICT in the teaching and learning processes in the Solomon Islands (Burns, 2000). Qualitative research relies on looking at the reasons behind various aspects of behaviour. It investigates the "why" and "how" of decision making, not just the "what", "where" and "when" (Cohen, Manion, & Morrison, 2007). As Malasa (2007) stated:

> Most traditional customs and beliefs are not written down or recorded but are mostly handed down from one generation to the next through an oral tradition. Therefore, it is important that any research carried out in the Solomon Islands be conducted within the participants' socio-cultural context. This is to ensure maximum participation and response from the research participants. (p. 50)

The study focused on secondary schools in Honiara, the capital city of the Solomon Islands. I assumed most schools there would have acquired some form of access to ICT tools. Furthermore, I chose to do my research in the city so as to have easy access to participants, and because I was constrained by a limited budget and research time. The schools are identified in this research as schools A, B, C and D. Three of the schools (A, B and C) are private schools and one is a public school (School D).

I selected eight technology education teachers (two from each school) from the four schools in Honiara, which all have access to computers and other ICT tools. I believed technology teachers in Honiara would be more familiar with ICT tools used in the school than their counterparts in rural schools. Furthermore, ICT is regarded as part of the technology education in the Solomon Islands, and so their views on and experiences with the integration of ICT tools in the school are relevant to my research. The participants were protected through a series of measures (assurance of anonymity and confidentiality) put in place to guard their identities. For the purposes of this discussion the participants are given pseudonyms.

Participants' profiles

These technology teachers teach technology education in Forms 1 to 5 and their teaching experience ranges from two years to more than 20 years. The participants are all male because there are very few women teaching technology in the Solomon Islands and they (female teachers) did not teach in the schools I visited. Participants held positions of class teacher, head of department and deputy principal. Six of the eight teachers were involved in the review of the national curriculum, which recently changed the industrial arts curriculum to a technology education curriculum. Their knowledge of the curriculum review and years of teaching experience helped them to explain the issues affecting the integration of ICT tools in the schools.

Data collection

The method of data collection used in the research was semistructured interviews. All interviews were conducted in both English and Solomon Islands pidgin. The parts of the interviews that were in pidgin were translated by the researcher and transcribed into English. To make sure the meaning was not lost in translation, the researcher returned the transcribed data to the participants and allowed them to check the meaning of their responses. With those who responded entirely in pidgin, the researcher went back to cross-check with them to ensure the translation represented what the participants actually said. This was possible because all the interviews were transcribed while the researcher was still in the research field. Each of the eight interviews took more than eight hours to transcribe. The researcher then went through each of the interviews more than once to check he had captured the meanings in the English translations.

Key findings

Limitations to access to and use of ICT in schools

A major issue raised by the technology teachers was the importance of access to and interaction with ICT tools in schools. Schools with well developed ICT integration are often the ones that provide sufficient access and use to their teachers and students. On the other hand, teachers' use of computers can be restricted by school policies. In some schools, access is limited or there is no organised time for teachers to use the computer lab and the Internet. In one school, teachers and students have the same time allocation each week to access computers in the computer lab, which restricts teachers' access to the tools. The teachers said that in most cases they gave priority to their students to use the computers in the lab. When they were asked why they would not use the lab with the students there, they said that the 14 computers in the lab were not enough for all the students and teacher together at one time.

Participants also said that because of the limited number of ICT tools in schools, teachers have to queue to use them. As a result, sometimes teachers just get frustrated and give up doing what they intended to do. This relates more to the use of computers than other ICT tools. Troy said that he would normally use the computer in the afternoon or evening because most other teachers would have gone home by then. In some schools only the principal and deputy principal have access to ICT tools, especially the computer. Clinton said that in his school, teachers cannot access the computers because they are kept in the principal's and deputy principal's offices. In school D only the secretary had access to ICT tools. James believed that such an arrangement restricts teachers from effectively using the tools as they would like, and limits their ability to design courses and teaching materials in the best possible way. When asked why the schools did not give teachers access to the computers and photocopy machines, participants said that they believed the school leaders did not want teachers to use the computers and photocopy machines because they were afraid the teachers might damage them due to their lack of knowledge and skills in using ICT tools.

Limited ICT infrastructure and resources in the schools and the impact on teacher use of ICT

ICT infrastructure and resources include computers, photocopy machines, the Internet, PowerPoint projectors, televisions, video players, printers and resources such as CD ROMs, websites and other ICT-prepared programmes for teaching. The types of ICT tools in the schools were limited. Although they may have computers, photocopy machines, printers, TVs, video recorders and digital cameras, and were connected to the Internet, most schools only have one or two ICT tools of each type. Table 1 below shows the number of ICT tools in each of the schools. When asked about their access to the Internet, participants said that the Internet is a new development in the Solomon Islands, and so not many schools are connected yet. Only two schools (private) out of the four schools visited have all the ICT tools outlined below and are also connected to the Internet. In the other two schools, a private (school C) and a public school, only basic ICT tools are available.

Table 1: The types and number of ICT tools teachers have access to in their schools

ICT tools	School				Total number of ICT tools
	A	B	C	D	
Computer	17	14	2 (plus 1 private)	2	36
Photocopy machine	2	1	1	1	5
Printer	2	2	1	1	6
TV and video recorder	1 set	1 set	1 set	1 set	4
Digital camera	1	1	1	0	3
Internet	broadband	broadband	0	0	2
PowerPoint projector	1	1	0	0	2
Fax machine	1	1	0	0	2
Mobile phone	Personally owned: not used for teaching and learning purposes				

Schools A and B are satisfactorily resourced with ICT tools. Technology teachers from these two schools said that the school managements provided leadership in making the adoption of ICT tools a reality. There was also a continuous process of strengthening ICT as an innovation for supporting teaching and learning through internal training and ICT access arrangements. However, while there seems to be a satisfactory level of ICT tools in schools A and B, the number of each type of ICT tool may not be sufficient for technology teachers to have access at any given time, let alone allowing use for the other teachers. A participant from one of the two schools highlighted this aspect:

> I think what we have now is very basic; we should acquire more ICT tools. If the school can afford to buy more ICT tools, I would like to see them buy PowerPoint projectors for us to use to improve our lesson delivery. At the moment, we have one projector but it is not enough for all of us; only the science department has access to it, not all of us. (Rendal)

On the other hand, schools C and D, a private and a public school, have a markedly inadequate number of ICT tools available. The reality of the state of ICT in most schools in the country is similar. Some schools, especially in the rural areas, may be worse off. The responses from the teachers at these two schools show that there are serious issues arising because of lack of ICT tools. For example, a participant in school C (private school) stressed the need for their school to purchase more computers for the teachers because they would queue for a long period of time just to gain access to the couple of computers in the school office.

Teachers' use of ICT tools

Technology teachers' use of ICT tools, as reported in this study, is minimal. Their personal interaction with ICT tools ranges from never having used them, to those who have gained a certain level of confidence using computers but are still in the process of learning. Four participants indicated that they had used the computer, printer, photocopier and the Internet. Six of the participants had used the computer and printer, and four the photocopier. Troy had used only the computer and printer. Although half the participants use the computer, printer, photocopier and the Internet, their experience was limited to basic uses such as word processing, direct copying of work and emailing. The table below summarises the types of ICT tools the participants have used.

Table 2: Types of ICT tools the participants have used

Participant	ICT tools
Talis	Computers, printers, photocopier, mobile phone (personal), the Internet
Rendal	Computers, printers, photocopier, mobile phone (personal), the Internet, PowerPoint projector, fax machine
Willie	Computer, printer, mobile phone (private), the Internet
Billy	Computers, printers, photocopier, the Internet
James	Has not used any ICT tools
Troy	Computer, printer
Gordon	Computers, printers, photocopier
Clinton	Mobile phone (personal)

Clinton had only used a mobile phone for personal use, while James had not used any ICT tools at all:

> To be honest I do not use ICT tools in my work. What I do is I give my work to the secretary to type for me so she is the one who uses the computer to do my job. (James)

> I do not use the computer or other ICT tools at all; I do not even play games on the computer. (Clinton)

The two quotes above are representative of a great number of teachers who have not used ICT tools in their work as a teacher. They are either teaching in a school where ICT has not yet been adopted, or they are in a school that has ICT tools but they lack the knowledge, skills or opportunity to learn how to use them.

Low level of ICT knowledge and skills

Another important finding was that the level of ICT knowledge and skills in the schools is very low. All the participants said that they needed ICT training in order to use ICT effectively in their teaching.

They reported that they learnt how to use the computer through the look-and-learn method and also by asking other teachers to show them how to use them. They all indicated that there is a lack of knowledge and skills in ICT among most teachers, and that acquiring basic skills on the computer and the photocopier was somewhat ad hoc.

Participants from school A, however, said that their school provides some formal training for the teachers and students, which helped teachers further understand how to use the computer and the Internet in their teaching. Unlike at school A, the majority of technology teachers in other schools lacked the knowledge and skills to help them properly integrate ICT into their teaching. This prevented them from fully maximising their potential as teachers. These teachers would have easily learnt how to use the computers if there was an arrangement in the schools that allowed them to spend time experimenting with using them or learning from those who know how to use them.

The need for policies on ICT use in schools

Most participants believed that when ICT is integrated into schools, there will be a need to put in place measures to guide teacher and student use. They believe that before any school acquires ICT tools, they must consider issues such as access for teachers and students, management and the appropriateness of ICT tools.

Rendal, James, Gordon and Willie highlighted the need for a policy to address the issue of using ICT tools appropriately, especially for educational purposes. Clinton, Rendal, Willie and Talis focused more on the aspects of the ICT tools, suggesting the ICT policy in education must address issues regarding the type, quality and ability of the tools to last a long time. They believed that such a policy would provide guidance to schools in acquiring appropriate ICT tools and help them to manage their use. Two of the participants indicated that before any commitment is made to buying ICT tools, it is important for a school to have a plan for their development. They viewed the whole integration process as a major innovation in teaching and learning. Rendal suggested that the Government should help schools to create their ICT development plans.

Participants also saw a need for controlling the access schools allowed teachers and students to the Internet. Gordon said that uncontrolled access to the Internet could provide the opportunity for access to undesirable materials and information, such as pornographic sites, or to resources not related to their official school work, such as movies, music and computer games. They suggested that guidelines for accessing the Internet should be put in place to control what users have access to. For example, James said:

> Control and guidance are also important for teachers' and students' use. They must be guided on what they can and can not access. This is to protect them from accessing pornographic websites and other similar materials. (James)

Teachers' beliefs about the benefits of ICT

Most of the participants believed teachers have much to benefit from ICT, that ICT tools had influenced their planning and that as a result of their basic skills in ICT they were now able to do their planning using the computer and save materials for future use. The participants also said that ICT has contributed to the enhancement of their teaching through having well prepared teaching materials. They believed that ICT would raise the level of their teaching if they acquired more knowledge and skills in using the tools. The limited experience they had in using ICT for various tasks in their teaching seemed to have a positive impact on the teachers' attitude to the benefits ICT offers. This made them believe that ICT can improve teaching and learning in the Solomon Islands. For example, Willie said that ICT had influenced most aspects of his teaching tasks, such as planning, preparing teaching materials and accessing resources on the Internet.

They also believed that by having access to ICT tools, students will have the opportunity to acquire resources that will broaden their learning opportunities. The participants felt that ICT can benefit students' learning through access to computers, the Internet and other types of ICT tools. They also said that ICT tools have contributed to students' understanding of lesson objectives because of the manner in which the learning tasks are organised and presented. However, this perception needs further verification, since I did not ask participants to show evidence of students' understanding of specific lesson objectives.

The need for professional development in ICT

Participants expected the Government, schools and education authorities to organise professional development in ICT use for teachers. They believed this would help teachers acquire the knowledge and skills needed to integrate ICT tools into their teaching. They identified several reasons for this:

- the current lack of knowledge and skills in using ICT for teaching and learning
- schools buying ICT tools without any prior training for teachers
- the changing nature of technology in the world today
- to enable schools to access information for teaching and students' learning.

These four issues make the need for professional development in ICT for teachers urgent. Participants associated the difficulties teachers encounter in their attempts to incorporate ICT tools in their teaching with a lack of professional development. They felt that the Government should provide ICT training as part of the integration of ICT in schools. They also suggested that ICT should be included as part of the teachers' training programme at the SICHE School of Education, which educates the majority of Solomon Islands teachers.

Significance of the findings

The findings raise a number of issues about teachers' access to ICT and their knowledge and skills in using it for teaching.

Teachers' access to ICT

The overwhelming finding from this study is that technology teachers have very limited access to ICT tools. Most of them reported only having access to the computer, printers, photocopier, mobile (personal) and the Internet. Teachers' level of ICT access is affected both by the availability of ICT in the schools and by how the schools organise the access. Many teachers did not have access, and also lacked the knowledge and the skills to use ICT tools because there was very limited ICT in their schools. This is consistent with the research of Almaghlouth (2008), BECTA (2004) and Earl (2002), who found that the lack of adequate ICT tools, and access to them, had prevented teachers from developing their skills.

Another important issue was the lack of an organised time or arrangement for teachers to use ICT tools in three of the schools visited. Teachers' chances to use an ICT tool seem to depend on the demand for the particular ICT tool on that day. The access that teachers should enjoy is not guaranteed, and this obstacle challenges teachers' desire to embrace ICT in their teaching (Guba, 2003). Teachers who have a strong desire to learn and use ICT tools have had to endure a variety of frustrations, such as having to negotiate access with their colleagues or having to wait patiently until the ICT tools are available for them to use. This is clearly seen in Troy's experience, when he said that he had to wait until everyone left for home in the afternoons before he could use the computer. ICT resources must be set up with schedules that allow ease of access for teachers, ICT training and ICT leadership, in both their use and development (BECTA, 2007).

Although schools A and B reported leadership commitment from the school principals to ICT integration, these principals could do more in their capacity as leaders of the schools to provide a satisfactory access strategy to the limited ICT resources they have. For example, school B received about nine new computers, but no one was creative and energetic enough to open the boxes and get somebody who knew how to install them to set them up for teachers to use. Similarly, school A's one-day access could easily be separated for teachers and students rather than allocating only three hours to both groups to share the 14 computers in the computer lab. Or the school could easily allocate two separate days: one for teachers and one for students. Such constraints will not create the opportunities described by Cowie et al. (2008) and Ham (2008), who both argue that sufficient teacher access to ICT tools in schools increases their confidence, understanding and skills in using ICT tools.

Schools C and D were far removed from any form of satisfactory leadership in terms of access for teachers and students to the limited ICT tools. Coupled with a very minimal number of ICT tools, there seemed to be no initiatives in place to give teachers the access they needed to the few computers, the photocopy machine and the printers they do have. This lack of leadership in integrating ICT tools in schools in the Solomon Islands is consistent with the findings of Balanskat, Blamire and Kefalla (2006), Earl (2002) and Healy (2003), who found that teachers are inhibited in developing ICT skills and knowledge because of factors such as unclear expectations and unclear roles and responsibilities in the integration of ICT tools in schools. For a school to satisfactorily integrate ICT tools, it requires forward-thinking leaders to provide leadership in setting clear expectations, roles and responsibilities for ICT development.

Teachers' use of ICT tools

My research shows that technology teachers use ICT tools more for administrative tasks than for teaching. Teachers use ICT tools to plan, prepare and word process curriculum materials, learning tasks and assessment instruments. In the findings, technology teachers highlighted administrative work. This is consistent with BECTA (2007, 2008), who said that teachers' views and practice have helped shape school planning in teaching, learning and curriculum delivery. The software most are familiar with is Microsoft Word. According to Smeets and Mooij (2001), teachers use word processing for their programmes, teaching materials, lesson instructions and learning tasks and activities. Other literature also suggests that the influence of ICT tools among teachers is limited by their competency level: a lack of competency influences how teachers use and interact with ICT tools (Ham, 2008; Spector & Anderson, 2000).

Teachers' level of ICT knowledge and skill

Although I did not expect to find a high level of ICT knowledge and skills among teachers, given that ICT is a new development in schools in the Solomon Islands, what I did expect was a scenario where teachers were supported and beginning to develop their skills in using ICT tools in their teaching. What I found was a mixed situation, where commitments made and measures taken were approached in a very ad hoc manner in terms of supporting teachers to develop their ICT knowledge and skills. Overall, the teachers' level of ICT knowledge and skills in the four schools visited was very low.

As discussed above, one of the reasons for such a prevalent lack of ICT knowledge and skills is the lack of sufficient ICT in the schools. This problem was confirmed by the overwhelming agreement among these technology teachers about the way in which they had acquired their basic knowledge and skills in ICT tools through the look-and-learn approach. Teachers, whether of technology or others, will definitely be lacking the sufficient knowledge and skills to help them effectively integrate ICT into their teaching in the Solomon Islands.

There is a link between the level of ICT knowledge and skills of teachers, and the availability of ICT tools in the schools. Teachers who are not provided with the opportunity to either use or have access to ICT are more likely to be lacking in ICT knowledge and skill (Pernia, 2008). The basic knowledge and skills the teachers have comes from their own personal interaction with each other. Proper co-ordination of ICT integration in the schools could bring about positive ICT knowledge and skills development for teachers.

Leeming (2003) has said that teachers in the Solomon Islands are not provided with training in ICT tools, which is consistent with what the participants in this study said in relation to their teacher training at SICHE's School of Education. In this situation, teachers will struggle to adapt to the use of ICT tools in teaching when schools decide to integrate ICT. Most of the teachers trained in the School of Education will be using a computer for the first time if they go to teach in a school with ICT.

The development of policies and guidelines for ICT use in schools

The need to protect students from accessing pornographic materials was seen by teachers as very important part of the integration of ICT in schools. They believe that if there are no control or guidelines put in place, students may abuse the access they have to the Internet. This issue is important to consider, because ICT integration in schools should provide the appropriate kind of learning, where students learn about their subject-related content. Filtering out pornographic materials from school Internet access is an essential part of ICT integration into schools. An Internet safety policy must include technology protection measures to block or filter Internet access to all kind of images that are obscene, promote pornography and/or are harmful to minors. Filtering school ICT access is also necessary because of the increase in Internet crime among young people (Grace & Kenny, 2003).

At the same time, teacher access to educational information related to sexual issues that are important for students to learn should not be filtered; for example, for subjects in the Solomon Islands curriculum that teach sexual health, human reproductive systems or maternal health. In this situation, access must be supported by written guidelines and teachers' supervision so that students are guided in exploring resources related to these areas of learning with ease. Control over what teachers can access from the Web must not carry the same restrictions as those put on students. This is out of respect for their professionalism and also in support of their status as teachers providing guidance to students.

There is also a need for school policies on computer placement and use. Deciding where to put the computers once they are purchased requires planning. Bialobrzeska and Cohen (2005) argue that whether a school has one computer or 100, the question of placement is equally important. Computers need to be installed in places where they are accessible to the people who can benefit from using them. A central location where teachers can easily have access is the staffroom. Three of the schools visited had computers and printers located in the staffroom, where teachers take turns to use them. However, the photocopy machine was located in the secretary's room, which in some cases might restrict teachers' access, especially when teachers work late at night. A central location in the school also provides easy access for all teachers. It provides a place where they can work and interact easily, and share their skills and knowledge so that they can learn from each other (Earl, 2002).

Future challenges

Technology teachers said that the benefit of ICT tools in teaching is that they make their work more efficient, organised and systematic. For example, teachers use the computer to prepare their curriculum notes and create files to store them, and print the document when they want to use it or make changes to it. PowerPoint makes their presentations clearer and more exciting for learners. Efficient work means teachers are able to access ICT tools when they want, can produce meaningful and clear teaching materials and are able to deliver or facilitate lesson instructions for their students. ICT tools can be beneficial to teachers in the development of their teaching tasks, curriculum work, instructional presentations and resourcing of students' learning (Leeming, 2003; Watson, 2001).

None of the four schools visited have enough ICT tools for their teachers to use at one time. Many teachers share the few computers that are available in the schools. Such scenarios cause frustration and loss of confidence for teachers, which means there are very few teachers who can use ICT in their schools. However, others are beginning to gain an interest in learning how to use them, and such a restrictive environment does not encourage teachers to pursue this.

The lack of sufficient ICT in schools prevents teachers from learning how to use ICT tools through the look-and-learn process, and to practise the skills they have learnt. Because of the demand for the few available ICT tools, many teachers do not have enough time to spend on them. Teachers wishing to do their work on the computer have to wait for the opportunity, which can take a long time. The effect of the lack of ICT in schools can be ineffective teaching and learning.

It is clear that most schools in the Solomon Islands do not have the resources to enable them to acquire adequate ICT for their schools. The challenge is too big a task for many schools to address alone. This is consistent with Pernia's (2008) report highlighting the struggle most developing countries face when they integrate ICT in education. Schools can easily appreciate the potential ICT offers, but they do not have the capacity to support the provision of ICT because of severe social and economic constraints. Schools may continue to buy ICT tools depending on their affordability. How effectively they integrate them into their schools will be a challenge for a while longer, until support is given to resource schools with sufficient ICT.

Conclusion

My research revealed that even technology teachers in my four study schools in Honiara had little opportunity to integrate ICT into their teaching. The schools lacked resources, access to ICT tools was variable and there was seldom any school planning. It seems that any integration of ICT in schools in the Solomon Islands has been solely due to the initiative taken by far-sighted school principals. While there are only a few schools in the Solomon Islands that have adopted the use of ICT, the trend (ICT integration) is gradually growing as schools plan to buy ICT tools such as computers, photocopy machines and digital cameras, and to connect to the Internet.

I believe that if ICT integration in Solomon Islands schools is to become reality there needs to be a well planned initiative by the Government, education authorities, school boards or the schools themselves. The Solomon Islands needs an education policy that guides the integration and use of ICT in education, since at present the country does not have a national ICT development strategy. Although workshops were held by the different government sectors to share ideas for setting up such a plan, no strategy has been put in place.

A national ICT policy would help determine requirements such as professional development for teachers, provide guidance for schools on how to integrate ICT tools properly and appropriately and how to manage ICT infrastructure and use in the schools. Technology is changing constantly, so a policy will help schools to identify which ICT tools are appropriate, for what purpose and what changes in technology they need to adopt.

References

Almaghlouth, O. A. D. (2008). *Saudi secondary school science teachers' perceptions of the use of ICT tools to support teaching and learning*. Unpublished master's thesis, University of Waikato, Hamilton.

Balanskat, A., Blamire, R., & Kefalla, S. (2006). *The ICT impact report: A review of studies of ICT impact on schools in Europe*. Retrieved from http://insight.eun.org/ww/en/pub/insight/misc/specialreports/impact_study.htm

BECTA. (2004). *A review of the research literature on barriers to the uptake of ICT by teachers*. Retrieved from http://partners.becta.org.uk/page_documents/research/barriers.pdf

BECTA. (2007). *Emerging technologies for learning*. Retrieved from http://partners.becta.org.uk/page_documents/research/emerging_technologies07.pdf

BECTA. (2008). *Harnessing technology review 2008: The role of technology and its impact on education*. Retrieved from publications.becta.org.uk/download.cfm?resID=38731

Bialobrzeska, M., & Cohen, S. (2005). *Managing ICTs in South African schools: A guide for school principals*. Retrieved from http://www.saide.org.za/resources/0000000108/Final_Saide_Layout(Screen).pdf

Burns, R. B. (2000). *Introduction to research methods* (4th ed.). Melbourne: Longman.

Cohen, L., Manion, L., & Morrison, K. (2007). *Research methods in education* (6th ed.). London: Routledge—Taylor & Francis Group.

Cowie, B., Jones, A., Hallow, A., McGee, C., Cooper, B., Forret, M., et al. (2008). *TELA: Laptops for teachers evaluation final report years 9–13*. Hamilton: University of Waikato.

Earl, K. (2002). *Curriculum innovation in a New Zealand secondary school: Identification of enablers and inhibitors*. Unpublished master's thesis, University of Waikato, Hamilton.

Grace, J., & Kenny, C. (2003). A short review of information and communication technologies and basic education in LDCs: What is useful, what is sustainable? *International Journal of Educational Development, 23*, 627–636.

Guba, S. (2003). *Are we all technically prepared?: Teachers' perspective on the causes of comfort or discomfort in using computers at elementary grade teaching*. Retrieved from http://www.accessmylibrary.com/coms2/summary_0286-23330460_ITM

Ham, V. (2008). *National trends in the ICT PD school cluster programme 2004–2006: Report to the Ministry of Education*. Retrieved from http://www.educationcounts.govt.nz/__data/assets/pdf_file/0017/22940/878_2004-NatTrends-ICTPD.pdf

Healy, D. (2003). *Enhancing subject-area expertise via the Internet: Advantages and limitations of computers and the internet for classroom teachers*. Retrieved from http://oregonstate.edu/~healeyd/upc/advdisadv.html

Leeming, D. (2003, November). *Education through wireless rural networking in Solomon Islands: The People First Network*. Paper presented at the 12th Asia Media and Information Communication Centre (AMIC) annual conference, Singapore.

Malasa, D. P. (2007). *Effective school leadership: An exploration of issues inhibiting the effectiveness of school leadership in Solomon Islands' secondary schools*. Unpublished master's thesis, University of Waikato, Hamilton.

MEHRD. (2004). *The national education action plan 2004–2006*. Honiara: Author.

MEHRD. (2007). *The national education action plan 2007–2009*. Honiara: Author.

Pernia, E. E. (2008). *Strategy framework for promoting ICT literacy in the Asia–Pacific region*. Bangkok: UNESCO.

Smeets, E., & Mooij, T. (2001). Pupil-centred learning, ICT, and teacher behaviour: Observations in educational practice. *British Journal of Educational Technology, 32*(4), 403–417.

Spector, J. M., & Anderson, T. M. (Eds.). (2000). *Integrated and holistic perspectives on learning and instruction: Understanding complexity*. Dordrecht, The Netherlands: Kluwer.

Watson, D. M. (2001). Pedagogy before technology: Re-thinking the relationship between ICT and teaching. *Education and Information Technologies, 6*(4), 251–266.

Solomon Pita

Solomon was born in Sasamungga village in Choiseul where he attended primary school. His secondary education was gained in Vonunu and Choiseul Bay Provincial Secondary School in Western Province and then at Goldie College. He was a member of the first diploma intake at the School of Education SICHE and then taught secondary technology for several years before completing his bachelors degree at the University of the South Pacific in 1999. He then returned to the School of Education as a lecturer until 2008 when he studied for and gained a masters degree in Education at the University of Waikato. Solomon is married with three children, is a keen rugby player and loves fishing.

CHAPTER 10
Attitudes to Inclusive and Special Education in the Solomon Islands

Janine Simi
School of Education, Solomon Islands College of Higher Education

Noeline Alcorn
University of Waikato

Introduction

The Solomon Islands Government, a signatory to the United Nations Convention on the Rights of the Child (ratified in 1995), has a responsibility to all children of the nation. Its *National Education Strategic Plan 2004–2006* (MEHRD, 2004) states that its aim is to "provide equitable access to services regardless of sex, ethnicity, ability or disability, location, economic status or age" (p.4.). The Government thus recognises the right and need of every person in society to be educated, and acknowledges that all students have the right to learn regardless of the nature, degree and complexity of their abilities or disabilities. Yet the *Solomon Islands National Disability Report* (Ministry of Health and Medical Services, 2005) provides evidence that many school-aged children with special needs are not gaining equal access and opportunity to attend school, even though most have expressed a desire to be educated. This report strongly suggests that the education system needs to develop frameworks to support and enhance special and inclusive education in the Solomon Islands. At present only two institutions, the Red Cross Special Development Centre and the Disability Centre, provide for students with disabilities.

The policy stance is an important step forward. However, the *National Strategic Action Plan* lacked clear guidelines for implementation; for example, it overlooked the need for the professional development of teachers and funding for schools if a unified system of integrating special needs children were adopted. One strategy was to establish formal training in special education at the School of Education, Solomon Islands College of Higher Education (SICHE), so that graduating students could return to their islands and villages with the appropriate knowledge, skills, practical ideas and resource materials. They would also be able to encourage children with special needs to attend their local schools, which would enable many of these children to enhance their self-esteem and social skills to become active members of their communities.

Since such training was at the very early planning stages, Janine decided to explore the attitudes, knowledge and understanding of special and inclusive education held by teachers' college students and staff. This would then become the basis for making more general recommendations about the implementation of inclusive education in the Solomon Islands. We argue in this chapter that such implementation demands the collaboration of stakeholders at all levels (from the school community to government), the development of clear policies and a commitment to make them happen.

The evolution of inclusive education

Until at least the mid-20th century education internationally for children with mental or sensory disabilities was carried out largely in specialised institutions or classes. Over time a growing number of parents and educators began to argue that all students, regardless of their abilities or disabilities, should be integrated into the mainstream of regular education. Such advocates believed there would be benefits to all children: they would learn to respect and value one another, despite their individual differences, and assist each other to learn (Fraser, Moltzen, & Ryba, 2005; Stainback, Stainback, & Forest, 1989).

Changes to cultural values, coupled with a human rights push for social justice, led to educational and legislative reforms to promote inclusive education. In June 1994 representatives of 92 governments and 25 international organisations formed the World Conference on Special Needs Education, convened by UNESCO and held in Salamanca, Spain. They agreed on a statement, which called for inclusive education to be the norm, and adopted a framework for action to try to ensure that all children would be able to attend their neighbourhood school, which would thus need to cater for widely diverse educational needs (UNESCO, 1994). This had huge implications for schools and school systems, which had to incorporate changes to their curriculum, organisation and resources, and were required to accommodate different styles and rates of learning. Inclusive education means that students with special needs are entitled to be educated, and their education should take place in regular settings (Macfarlane, 2007).

Inclusive education also required a paradigm shift in the underlying theoretical assumptions about learning. From the 19th century special education had been based on a medical theory, which held that learning problems and deviant behaviours are the result of organic disorder, disease or impairment within the individual. This was challenged by Bronfenbrenner (1979), whose ecological theory suggests that development takes place through interaction with others and the environment, and who advocated a more holistic approach. Whereas the aim of earlier educators had been to help children with disabilities to fit into the existing educational environment, the new paradigm insists that educators need to alter their beliefs and adapt the environment to meet the needs of all children.

The success of inclusive education depends very much on teachers' perceptions and attitudes. Several studies have found that teachers hold negative views about inclusive education (Jangira & Scrinivasan, 1991), or are unwilling to teach students with special needs in their classrooms even though they support inclusive education (Scruggs & Mastropieri, 1996). Head teachers and administrators were found to be more positive than classroom teachers (Norwich, 1994). Forlin (1995) found that special education teachers, on the other hand, were positive, partly because they were trained in the area and had continuous interaction with special needs children. General teachers lacked confidence in their ability to cater for diverse needs in an inclusive setting without specific knowledge and skills, and felt they worked with no training, resources or funding. Also, some parents of children with disabilities feared general teachers lacked the skills and training to work inclusively, and focused too heavily on academic education at the expense of life skills.

As a result of these findings, researchers have advocated that both initial teacher education and inservice professional development programmes should contain courses that equip teachers with the skills and knowledge to implement inclusive education in their classrooms (Foreman, 2005; Fraser et al., 2005; Hodgkinson, 2005). Classroom organisation is important, together with strategies such as co-operative learning and peer tutoring, which help students to develop interpersonal communication skills (Johnson, Johnson, & Holubec, 1994; Slavin, 1990; Smith, Polloway, Patton, & Dowdy, 2004).

Experience in New Zealand has demonstrated that governments, schools and training institutions need to work together to formulate policies that will support inclusive education. There needs to be a policy commitment to guide implementation while supporting national educational goals. In New Zealand this is provided by the Education Act 1989 and the Human Rights Act 1993, and by the Special Education 2000 policy (Ministry of Education, 1998). The Solomon Islands has provided such a framework in the *National Education Strategic Plan 2004–2006* (MEHRD, 2004) and the *Solomon Islands National Disability Report* (Ministry of Health and Medical Services, 2005). But policies cannot operate effectively without funding. Fraser et al. (2005) have stated that the goals of inclusive practices in schools cannot be achieved without government funding to provide resources, teacher aides and other support. At the same time policies need the genuine support of school leaders to champion inclusion, communicate with parents and provide support for teachers and students.

Background to this study

As indicated earlier, one of the strategies included in the *National Disability Report* and the *National Education Strategic Plan* was the development of training programmes that prepare teachers to work in inclusive classrooms. Given the importance of attitudes towards and understanding of inclusive education, if the processes are to be successfully implemented, investigating the perspectives, knowledge and beliefs held by those preparing to teach in Solomon Islands schools is a vital step before formal preparation courses can be developed. As a staff member of the School of Education, Janine had a keen interest in ensuring that new developments were soundly based on evidence.

This study investigated such perceptions through semistructured interviews with three teacher educators and eight second-year teacher education students enrolled at the School of Education, SICHE. The interviews were carried out in pidgin, and so the tapes had to be transcribed and translated into English without losing meaning and precision. A focus group involving the students was held later. Seven of the students had completed Year 11 schooling before entering the college, and one had completed Year 12. Two of the School of Education staff held master's degrees and the third had a postgraduate qualification. Five respondents were male and six female. To protect their anonymity the students are referred to as P1–8 and their gender is indicated by the addition of M or F. Lecturers are referred to as P1–3/L.

Perceptions of special and inclusive education among teacher education students and teacher educators

All 11 participants were able to provide definitions of special education as it relates to educating those with disabilities and other needs, but the idea of inclusive education was quite new to the students. One representative comment was, "I don't know. I have never come across that concept during the course of my training here at this college" (P1/F). The teacher educators were able to give definitions, though not from experience:

> Inclusive education is an approach whereby children with special needs should be included in all aspects of development in the society. That would also involve including them into our school system and letting them into our classrooms. At the moment, there is not provision for children with special needs in our current school and education system. (P2/L)

> Inclusive education would be education that serves to meet the needs of every child in the regular classroom despite their abilities or disabilities, background, talent, etc. (P3/L)

With one exception, both groups were positive about the concept. A student teacher commented:

> I can see that inclusive education is a good concept and I believe it is high time that our schools became inclusive because we have many children with special needs living amongst us in our communities that are accessing education. (P6/M)

One participant, however, felt its introduction was premature:

> I feel that it is not yet appropriate to introduce this concept of inclusion because currently teacher educators are not well equipped with skills and knowledge on inclusion. More so, I would like to see that students with special needs go to their special schools first so that they can be prepared before coming into regular classrooms with their helper. (P3/M)

Not surprisingly, the teacher education students did not feel they had developed any skills and knowledge on inclusive education and had very limited knowledge and general information on special education. They did not feel confident about their capacity to cope with teaching a child with special needs in their classrooms. The teacher educators acknowledged that neither area was covered:

> No! Currently we only offer general education to the preservice teacher based on the demand of the 'normal' general population. At the moment, only very little is covered in terms of basic knowledge on what is special education. (P2–L)

Although they all acknowledged that there were children in their villages with special needs, seven of the eight teacher education students indicated that they had not seen any in the schools they attended during their practicum. When asked why they thought these special needs children were not attending school, they responded that parents might not think they need to go as they would not learn anything. The students also thought these children might not be welcomed by teachers and other students, and that there were negative cultural attitudes towards them:

> Other normal children at school will tend to tease this group of children, thus causing them to shy away from school. On the other

hand, schools and classrooms are not welcoming to this group of children in terms of their design, programmes and facilities. (P5/F)

A teacher educator explained:

Culturally those with obvious physical disabilities are seen as a form of curse upon the person and the family. Maybe they have made the traditional gods and ancestors unhappy and as a result a child has been born with disabilities to punish the family. This negative cultural misunderstanding goes on the child. In the end nobody will want to have anything to do with that child for fear that the curse will fall upon them as well. (P2/L)

Participants were clear that action to foster positive steps to address the situation were possible. Students suggested that schools should establish better relationships with parents and educate communities on the rights of children with disabilities to attend school. They accepted that within their own classrooms they could welcome special needs children and work to make their environments more interesting. Teacher educators saw the need for better co-ordinating mechanisms among stakeholders, and for promoting links between their communities and education authorities. Schools need to provide facilities and amenities to cater for the needs of all children, but one noted that the country lacks money to build special facilities for special needs. Both groups believed school leaders play a crucial role. They acknowledged that because the School of Education had no policy statement on inclusive education, it was not part of the curriculum.

Once the needs were made obvious to them, the students began to generate ideas for ameliorating the situation. In a focus group held after the interviews were completed, they put forward a range of ideas. They believed schools should work together with parents, and that schools and teachers should forge links with the two special schools in the Solomon Islands. In addition, they suggested there was a need to review the current education system to cater for inclusion.

Not only did they suggest preservice training, they also wanted schools to carry out more awareness programmes on special and inclusive education with villages and communities.

Issues arising from the findings

The findings confirmed that teacher education students had limited understanding of special education and that "inclusive education" was an unknown term. Their answers to questions about special education indicated that they were aware only of children with disabilities. Teacher educators, on the other hand, with broader experience in education, had a fair understanding of what inclusive education involved, but they had not shared this understanding with their students. Nevertheless, both groups expressed positive views about inclusion once the concept was explained.

International research has found that if special needs children are to be successfully integrated into inclusive schools and classrooms, their teachers need the skills to enable them to modify their curricula for children with diverse abilities (Loreman, Deppler, & Affleck, 2005; Smith et al., 2004). Such training will provide confidence and allay the anxiety that inclusive education is too difficult. But the teacher education students in the study lacked both confidence and knowledge, and the teacher educators felt there was not sufficient time to include such material in their courses. It will be important for the School of Education to consider carefully how to provide at least some information and understanding to their pre-service students.

The interview data suggested that although there are a number of children with special needs living in the villages in the Solomon Islands, most of them are not attending school. This finding is consistent with the *Solomon Islands National Disability Report* (Ministry of Health and Medical Services, 2005), which found that existing schools cannot accommodate such children in terms of services and facilities. In spite of this, one student had noted children with visual and hearing impediments attending school. It will be important for the Ministry of Education and Human Resources Development (MEHRD) to ensure more thorough research into this issue is carried out.

My study attempted to discover why students with special needs were not attending school. One reason was cultural conceptions about disability. There is a strong belief in Solomon Islands culture that there is a metaphysical cause of physical disability, which involves an attempt to explain why such disability has occurred. Studies in Tanzania (Kisanji, 1993) and India (Dalal & Pande, 1999) also mention such cultural beliefs about the causes of disability. Such beliefs haunt the disabled person and cause him or her to be perceived differently by members of the society and community. It seems that the Solomon Islands as a country and society needs to start working towards developing a change of mind-set and beliefs about how it perceives those with special needs. Being born with a physical deformity is not the result of supernatural powers. Instead of being negative towards these people, parents, teachers, government officials, institutions and society in general need to offer support and help. It is particularly important for parents to feel that their children with special needs have a right to the same degree of education as other children and should not be hidden away.

If this is to occur, then schools must become more welcoming and more adapted to the diverse needs of students. It was reported that special needs children were not attending school because their needs could not be accommodated. Schools in the Solomon Islands have been designed to suit the general population without taking into consideration those with special needs. For example, there is no evidence of ramps or other facilities. More importantly, however, teachers have not been trained to employ strategies such as co-operative learning and peer tutoring, which have been demonstrated to contribute to the academic achievement of special needs children (Fraser et al., 2005; Johnson et al., 1994; Slavin, 1990).

A possible way forward

Since inclusive education is a new concept in the Solomon Islands, there is a need for long-term planning to facilitate its introduction into schools. Goodwill, such as that expressed by the teacher education students in their focus group, will not be sufficient. This is a worldwide challenge. A report by the United Nations Educational, Scientific and Cultural Organisation (UNESCO) in 2002 identified one of the greatest problems threatening the world today as the growing number of persons who are being excluded from meaningful participation in the economic, social and cultural life of their communities.

The need in the Solomon Islands is great. Currently there are only two schools in the country catering specifically for children with disabilities: the Red Cross Special Development Centre and the Disability Support Centre for the Blind. Both are in Honiara, and children in rural areas have little chance to access them. This makes planning for inclusive education more imperative, to provide an avenue through which all children with special needs in the country can participate in education.

A multipronged approach is needed. At the grass-roots level it is important that schools and communities collaborate so that parents are aware of the inclusive philosophy. This links to evidence that inclusive education needs to be "rooted well" in the minds of parents and communities to be successful (Loreman et al., 2005; Smith et al., 2004). This puts an expectation on schools to be in the front line in carrying out awareness programmes, and accentuates the need for teachers to be provided with the appropriate understanding and skills. The eventual outcome should be for villages and communities to understand the rights of every child to education.

Schools have a big role to play in the dissemination of information. If schools are to play such an educative role, then principals need to exercise significant leadership in supporting teachers. As Macfarlane (2006) asserts, sound inclusive practices depend on leaders with vision who are able to identify and address problems in an appropriate manner and work well with others. This is an important challenge for leaders in the Solomon Islands.

Schools can only play this role effectively if there is a policy framework to guide the delivery of special and inclusive education. Although the Solomon Islands Government has recognised the need to provide basic education for all children in its *National Education Strategic Plan 2004–2006*, this document is very broad and has limited coverage in the area of special and inclusive education. The School of Education at SICHE is mandated through the Education Act 1982 to provide training for teachers, but it places most importance on training for general education, to the extent that students had not even heard of inclusive education. Including special and inclusive education in its mission statement would be a step forward.

The study also revealed a lack of government funding to support special and inclusive education. Indirectly this may suggest that special and inclusive education is not a priority for the Government, and that a change of mind-set will be needed so that funding can be provided to drive the area forward. The findings of this research study point to the need for both the Government, through the MEHRD, and the School of Education to give greater emphasis to this important issue.

The major recommendation arising from this study is the need for strong links between all stakeholders—the MEHRD, the School of Education, schools, parents and communities—to facilitate inclusiveness in Solomon Islands education. The model below (see Figure 1) summarises the possibilities.

Figure 1: Possible model for inclusive education in the Solomon Islands

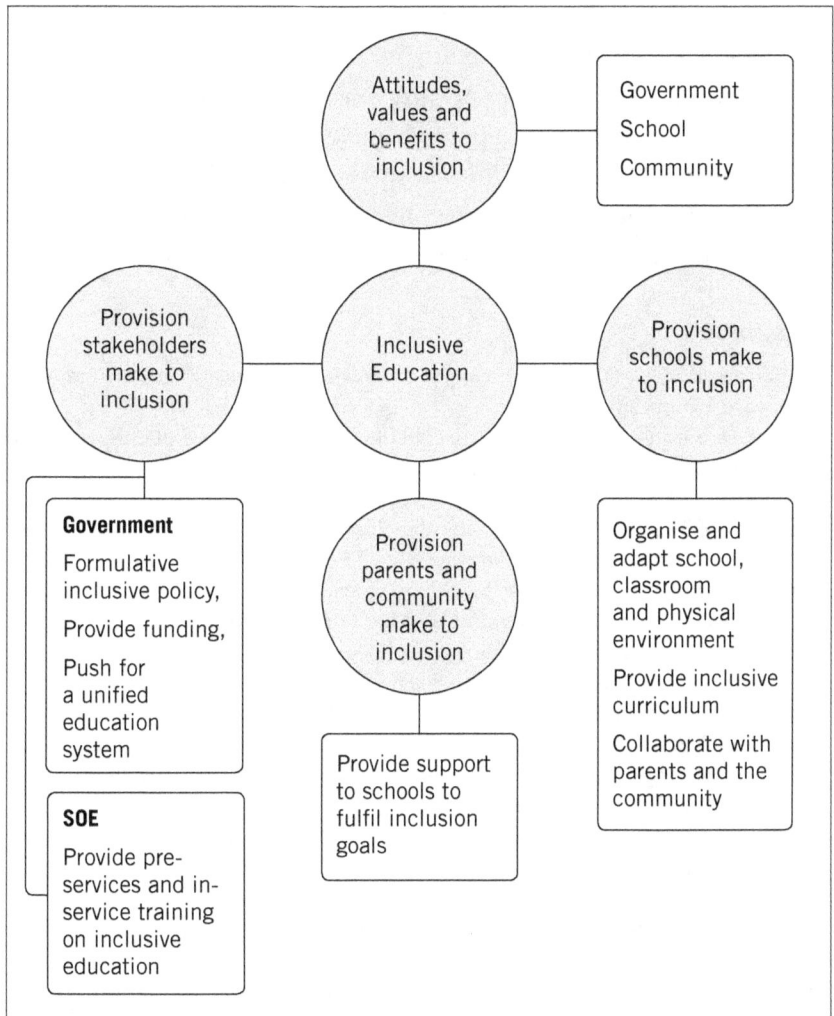

This model of inclusion involves a set of interconnecting parts that make up the whole. It can develop from the top down or vice versa. Clearly, attitudes, values and beliefs must be at the heart of the thinking of decision makers in the Government, the community and, ultimately, the schools. Key stakeholders must formulate policies that push for a unified education system and provide preservice and inservice training on inclusive education. Other groups in the community must offer support to schools to implement these policies. Collaboration with parents and community is an important part of the whole process. Ultimately it is the schools and teachers in our society that bear the responsibility. Inclusive education is not just an ideal. It must become a reality for our children and our society.

References

Bronfenbrenner, U. (1979). *The ecology of human development.* Cambridge, MA: Harvard University Press.

Dalal, A., & Pande, N. (1999). Cultural beliefs and family care of children with disability. *Psychology and Developing Societies, 11,* 1.

Foreman, P. (2005). *Inclusion in action.* Southbank, VIC: Thomson.

Forlin, C. (1995). Educators' beliefs about inclusive education practices in Western Australia. *Journal of Special Education, 22,* 179–185.

Fraser, D., Moltzen, R., & Ryba, K. (2005). *Learners with special needs in Aotearoa New Zealand* (3rd ed.). Palmerston North: Dunmore Press.

Hodgkinson, A. (2005). Conceptions and misconceptions of inclusive education: A critical examination of final-year teacher trainees' knowledge and understanding of inclusion. *Research in Education, 73,* 15–28.

Jangira, N., & Scrinivasan, K. (1991). Attitudes of educational administrators and teachers towards education of disabled children. *Indian Journal of Disability and Rehabilitation,* July–December, 25–35.

Johnson, W., Johnson, R., & Holubec, J. (1994). *Cooperative learning in the classroom.* Alexandria, VA: Association for Supervision and Curriculum Development.

Kisanji, J. (1993). *Special education in Africa.* London: Kogan Page.

Loreman, T., Deppler, J., & Affleck, J. (2005). *Inclusive education: A practical guide to supporting diversity in the classroom.* New York: RoutledgeFalmer.

Macfarlane, A. (2006). *Theoretical models in special education.* [lecture notes], University of Waikato, Hamilton.

Macfarlane, A. (2007). *The importance of research in education.* [lecture notes], University of Waikato, Hamilton.

MEHRD. (2004). *National education strategic plan 2004–2006.* Honiara: Author.

Ministry of Education. (1998). *Special education 2000: Getting it right together.* Wellington: Author.

Ministry of Health and Medical Services. (2005). *Solomon Islands national disability report.* Honiara: Author.

Norwich, D. (1994). The relationship between attitudes to the integration of children with special needs and a wider socio-political view: A US–English comparison. *European Journal of Special Educational Needs, 9*, 91–106.

Scruggs, T., & Mastropieri, M. (1996). Teachers perceptions of mainstreaming/inclusion 1985–1996: A research synthesis. *Exceptional Children, 63*(1), 59–74.

Slavin, R. (1990). *Cooperative learning, theory, research and practice.* Upper Saddle River, NJ: Prentice Hall.

Smith, T., Polloway, E., Patton, J., & Dowdy, C. (2004). *Teaching students with special needs in inclusive settings* (4th ed.). New York: Pearson Education.

Stainback, W., Stainback, S., & Forest, M. (1989). *Educating all students in the mainstream of the regular classroom.* London: Paul H. Brookies.

UNESCO. (1994). *The Salamanca statement and framework for action on special education needs.* Paris: Author.

Janine Simi

Janine was born in Papua New Guinea on the island of Bouganville where she attended village primary schools. Her secondary schooling took place at Betikama Adventist School in Guadalcanal and at King George VI school. After school she worked for the Ministry of Agriculture and Lands, then enrolled at SICHE where she completed a Diploma of Physical Planning in the School of Natural Resources. Following that she moved to Australia to study for a Bachelor of Education at Griffith University. After graduation she returned to Honiara to teach English, social studies and senior geography at King George VI College. Some years later she took up a position as Lecturer in Education at the School of Education, SICHE. She completed a masters degree in Education at the University of Waikato and returned to the School of Education. She was appointed Head of School in 2010. Janine is married with three children and her interests include gardening and family outings.

Noeline Alcorn

Noeline is an Emeritus Professor of Education at the University of Waikato. She was Dean of the School of Education from 1992-2006 and has been associated with the partnership from the beginning. Her publications are mainly in history and policy studies in education. She has supervised many student theses.

www.ingramcontent.com/pod-product-compliance
Lightning Source LLC
Chambersburg PA
CBHW081330230426
43667CB00018B/2884